It's Never Too Soon

It's NEVER TOO SOON

DR. RUTH PETERS

Golden Books
New York

Golden Books®
888 Seventh Avenue
New York, NY 10106

Designed by Suzanne Noli

Manufactured in the United States of America

10 9 8 7 6 5 4 3 2 1

Library of Congress Cataloging-in-Publication Data

Peters, Ruth Allen.
    It's never too soon / Ruth Peters.
      p. cm.
    Includes bibliographical references and index.
    ISBN 0-307-44002-8 (alk. paper)
    1. Discipline of children. 2. Child rearing. 3. Parenting.
  4. Parent and child. I. Title.
HQ770.4.P46645   1998
649'.64—dc21   98-2880
                                        CIP

To my family—my little piece of heaven.

CONTENTS

It's Never Too Soon

INTRODUCTION:
DISCIPLINE MEANS "TEACHING"

"Discipline"—just hearing the word sends chills down the spines of many parents. "Must I really punish this child if she gets into things?" laments the mother of a two-year-old. I believe the word "discipline" has been given a bad rap. It connotes punishment, criticism, and correction—all negative-sounding words. However, discipline is not negative at all; in fact, it is a very positive concept. Discipline means "teaching," pure and simple, using a combination of explanation, reasoning, and action to train a child to understand what behaviors are acceptable or unacceptable. It definitely does not mean abuse, although many parents jump to the conclusion that disciplining a child involves reprimand, spanking, or criticism. Unfortunately, in some homes, the majority of disciplinary tactics may be just that—negative or harsh words, screaming, or smacking. The enlightened parent, though, has many other disciplinary tools to choose from that are not only more humane, but actually much more effective.

Your reaction to your child's inappropriate behaviors teaches her the consequences of her actions. If you generally react with harsh words or physical punishment, she'll get the idea her mom and dad don't like what she's just done, and they believe in physical aggression to solve problems. This type of discipline may or may not change the child's behavior, but it will most likely lead to an angry child, or to one who may grow immune to being screamed at or clobbered. In my more than twenty years of experience as a psychologist working with kids and their parents, I've met lots of folks who swear that they had to spank their kids hard or say awful things in order to get their attention. Even so, many have come to the conclusion that it's just not worth it. Kids tend to repeat the behavior they were spanked for, and parents feel rotten about themselves for frightening their children with a spank.

I've also worked with many families in which the kids have confided to me that the nonaggressive disciplinary tactics that I teach to their parents actually "hurt" more than being yelled at or spanked. These humane, effective tactics definitely get the kid's attention and teach him to change the offensive behavior.

T. Berry Brazelton, in his excellent book *Touchpoints: Your Child's Emotional and Behavioral Development,* notes that "next to love, a sense of discipline is a parent's second most important gift to a child." Helping children learn self-discipline—understanding and accepting life's limits and behaving accordingly—is key. Brazelton notes that self-discipline in the toddler and young child evolves through three stages: testing the limits by exploratory behavior, "teasing" others to check out whether the behavior is appropriate or not, and—once he learns his parent's reaction—internalizing the new boundaries. The toddler who is firmly told no as he touches the button on the television and is then moved to the other side of the room quickly learns to expect to be reprimanded and moved away from the forbidden object. Within a few months, the child himself says no as he touches the television, removes his hand by himself, and looks around for his parent's reaction. Why? Because he has learned the connection between his behavior (touching the television set) and his parent's response (firm verbal reprimand and being placed away from the object).

This stimulus (touching)–response (discipline) connection, which will occur thousands of times within the first six years of life, teaches him the boundaries of acceptable behavior. Babies, toddlers, young children, teens, and even adults continue to need to be taught what the acceptable limits of behavior are. Children who are not given this knowledge continue to exceed the boundaries, either because they have not been taught limits by their parents or because the boundary lines have consistently changed. Some of these children tend to be anxious and unsure of themselves. Others become aggressive and out of control as they look for limit setting from their elders.

How many times do you remember noticing your child, even as a baby, looking at you as he is about to perform a forbidden behavior, such as touching the crystal vase or ripping a magazine? He's looking at you to see what your reaction will be. If he gets none, he won't learn to remove his hand, and most likely will continue to engage in the forbidden behavior. If your reaction is inconsistent (sometimes you reprimand, other times you ignore his behavior), he'll become confused and his behavior may range from timidity to aggression as he tries to figure out by himself what is appropriate (a difficult task for a toddler or young child to perform). If you consistently discipline (perhaps removing him from the situation), he'll quickly get the picture. He may not like the consequence and he may not even like you at the moment for putting him in time-out, but he will have taken one small step toward self-discipline. He'll learn that his behavior (both appropriate and inappropriate) leads to definite consequences (both good and bad) and he has the power to determine what the end result will be.

By the time he is six years of age, your son will have had thousands of opportunities to learn the connection between his behavior and your response. If the connection is clear, he'll most likely be making appropriate choices (of course, with occasional trips outside the limits). His history of externally controlled discipline, in the form of parental guidance, will begin to become internally based through this behavior–response connection. And that is the essence of teaching self-discipline, which I believe to be one of the most important goals of parenting.

If your child can make this connection by age six, he'll most likely be able to maintain it through the rest of his school years. He'll travel into adulthood secure that he understands and accepts life's rules, and because of this knowledge and self-control, he'll be productive and satisfied as an adult. Kids who have not been given the gift of self-discipline often grow up to be disappointed, ill-behaved teenagers and adults. They forever blame others for their lack of success and perseverance, and are often quite miserable.

So when your baby crawls to the television, reaches for the button, and looks to you for your reaction, think of this as a lesson in Self-Discipline 101, and begin to teach the lesson. If you don't, he'll learn nothing from class that day, but if you discipline him, he's not only learning to control his impulse to touch the forbidden object, he's also beginning his voyage toward making the behavior–consequence connection, one of the most important journeys of his life!

Decisions, Decisions . . .

At a very young age, your baby will present you with problem situations (or opportunities to teach, depending upon your perception) in which you must make decisions about how to respond. Letting the baby sleep in your bed in order to get her to be quiet, picking her up at the first whimper rather than waiting to see if she can calm down on her own, or constantly playing fetch for dropped spoons or toys are challenges that most parents have to deal with from the very beginning.

How you manage these situations will have an immediate effect upon your child. Habits such as refusing to sleep in the crib, demanding to be held all the time, or constantly throwing objects to get and keep your attention are very quickly learned. Many of these behaviors can become habits after just a few experiences.

In my clinical psychology practice, I've counseled hundreds of parents on how to deal with these and other typical baby, toddler, and young child issues. Philosophically, there are no right or wrong answers. I tell my clients that if they don't mind Junior sleeping in bed with them every night, then it's okay to start the habit. Or if they like the feel of twenty-five extra pounds of baby hanging on their left hip most of the day, then it's fine to pick the child up at the first whimper. None of these behaviors *alone* will permanently damage the kid's psyche—in fact, the child will probably appreciate sleeping in your warm bed at night or having you at her mercy all day—but you may go nuts! Having a baby in bed is fun for the first few minutes—he's so cute, he probably smells good at the moment, and that smile. To die for! Knowing that all you have to do to quiet your little one is to pick him up may make you feel good at first, but it gets old when you're also trying to juggle the mail and grab the groceries at the same time.

My point is that these early behaviors are partially baby control tactics (yes, even little ones can be manipulative). Baby is not aware of the coup that he is pulling off; he's just doing what works. I guarantee that he won't whimper to be held in the ninth grade or desire to sleep in your bed as a middle schooler—these behaviors will go away.

But baby will learn other manipulative tactics as she grows older, such as provoking guilt in order to get her way, engaging in out-of-control behavior, or talking back. In effect, you are teaching your child at an early age that she's the one in control of the situation, not you.

The real test of parenting begins at around the child's first birthday. By twelve months of age, kids can make lots of relationship connections: If I spit out the green stuff, Dad will cave in and give me crackers. If I holler loud enough while Mom's talking on the phone, she'll hang up and come play with me. Smart kids, these babies and toddlers—a lot sharper than we give them credit for.

Baby keepsake books leave lots of space to write down the particulars of baby's first step or first words. It would be helpful, not to mention interesting, if they also allowed room for parents to jot down baby's first control tactic and their response to it. Parents could document the manipulations their child is prone to, even as young as eight weeks of age. If parents were to look back, there definitely would be a pattern. Some kids will employ the dependent, help-me routine, in which Mom and Dad have to do things for their eighteen-month-old that she obviously can do for herself, such as reaching certain toys or feeding herself. Other toddlers are pros at keeping their parents on edge, afraid that if they don't let Junior have exactly what he wants, exactly when he wants it, he'll reward them with a temper tantrum off the Richter scale.

What's a parent to do about all this misbehavior? First, realize that your kid is probably smarter than you think. And more determined. And not especially concerned with social etiquette. And relatively ego-centric, as in "I want what I want when I want it!" Once you've accepted that babies, toddlers, and preschoolers can be crafty, you're halfway home.

The next step is to look inside yourself to understand your personal parenting agenda. What "rules" of parenting did you grow up with? Who were your role models? What did you say you'd never do or always do as a parent? How guilt-prone are you? Do you take respon-sibility for others' feelings, their sadness, resentment, loneliness? Do you believe that your child should be happy most of the time, and that it's your responsibility to see to that? Understanding your parent-ing agenda is critical to understanding how and why you respond to your children's behavior.

Kids are born with distinct and persevering personality styles— difficult babies who never seem to be satisfied and are described as edgy and easily disturbed; easy babies who seem to roll with the punches, napping in the middle of karate class or Mom's haircut ap-pointment; and slow-to-warm-up kids who are threat-sensitive and faithfully clingy. How you react to your child's actions, though, can mold her behavior and personality to a large degree. This is the nature (what baby is born with)–nurture (how the environment affects baby) debate that has been studied by developmental psychologists for de-cades. Most studies have shown that the combination of nature and nurture is what colors your child's growth, disposition, and develop-ment.

You can do nothing about the nature side; your child's genetic traits (hair color, body shape, and some personality characteristics) are predetermined. It's the nurture part that can modify the type of per-son your child will grow to be. Just as a youngster who is "wired" for obesity can be kept to a normal weight through dietary and exercise regimens, a genetically touchy, edgy kid can be taught patience and self-control if his parents work with him on these behaviors and atti-tudes as he matures. He'll probably never be as easygoing as his older sister, who was born genetically predisposed to a laid-back attitude, but he can be taught self-control and to be more tolerant of disappointments.

This book will lead you through the parenting styles and tactics that I've found work best with the various types of personalities and behaviors of kids ages three to seven. I've worked with hundreds of families of preschoolers and kindergartners and found that at some point most have a need for a "behavioral tune-up," or even a major overhaul, to get their kids back on track and Mom and Dad parenting effectively again. The behavior management programs I suggest are effective and make the child-rearing years more fun and rewarding for all—both parents and kids. My own kids have grown up with a behavior management system as part of their lives—which changes and evolves as they grow older. Realizing that their behavior leads to clear and definite consequences has helped my children to usually make the right choices and decisions. Of course, there are occasional "blips" on the screen, but they've turned out to be terrific kids who abide by our rules.

And this, I believe, is the basis of raising good children. Kids who learn to accept and expect defined consequences for their behavior (if you do as you're told, you can have more privileges) understand the concept of personal responsibility. It makes sense to them, and they do not see a need to defy it or avoid responsible behavior as adults. They adjust to society's values and learn to accept that one doesn't always get one's way, a characteristic that becomes very important later in social and work situations. In essence, they learn to become reasonable and rational—but they must learn these lessons from you, their parent. This type of parenting is not always an easy road to follow, and there have been many times when it's taken all of my creativity and tenacity to outsmart a strong-willed, manipulative child. But in the end I know that it's well worth it!

1
UNDERSTANDING THE STAGES OF DEVELOPMENT

Babies are born almost totally helpless, dependent upon their caretaker to feed them, keep them warm and comfortable, and to love them. The baby is the center of not only his universe, but also of yours. The newborn's only way to make his needs known is to cry, scream, and flail his arms and legs. In newborns, we accept these behaviors as signals for attention or help. In the two-year-old, however, we describe these same behaviors as temper tantrums. Why the difference? Because newborns have not yet developed alternative ways of communicating their needs other than crying. They're not neurologically nor experientially mature enough to do so. But a two-year-old can usually express himself well enough verbally to make his needs and desires clear, and we often expect him to do just that—tell us just what it is he needs or wants. And to complicate matters, we often expect the preschooler to accept our decision even if it is the opposite of what he desires.

Sounds reasonable enough at first glance—babies who can't verbalize are expected to cry, whereas two-year-olds who can speak are expected to talk and go along with the program. We believe that reasoning should work. After all, we say, "She does understand what I'm telling her. It makes perfect sense. So why is she throwing such a fit?"

The answer is twofold. First, what makes *sense* to an adult is often seen as *nonsense* to a preschooler. Second, adult priorities tend to be complex, built upon years of experience and knowledge of cause-and-effect relationships. But preschoolers tend to live in the moment—easily forgetting (and therefore not learning from) the past, and with little concern for the future. That's normal little-kid human nature. You can, though, lessen your youngster's degree of egocentricity and help mold his priorities by providing the right atmosphere in your home.

A window of opportunity to teach emotional and behavioral responsibility occurs around the child's first birthday. However, most parents miss it, still assuming that the baby cannot be held responsible for her emotions and behaviors. Instead of considering discipline, many of us continue to placate, distract, or give in to a tantrumming child. In fact, in many homes, parents consider disciplining only after the child's second birthday. Think of that. The child is allowed at least two years of uncontrolled emotional outbursts without consequence! However, babies can learn how to handle their upsets more appropriately much earlier than many parents expect, and to deprive them of this learning opportunity is a shame. Few parents would consider not teaching their kids the alphabet, because it's obvious that they'll need this knowledge in kindergarten. Why is it less important to teach your toddler self-control?

I believe the problem lies in what parents feel to be acceptable child-rearing priorities. Many consider baby- and toddlerhood to be a behavioral free-for-all—a time to cuddle, have fun with, and love your child unconditionally. Cuddling is great, but babyhood should also be a time to begin teaching the lessons inherent in limit setting. There is no conflict in loving your baby while beginning to teach him boundaries and responsibilities. Both can and should be done simultaneously.

Every family is different and, therefore, disciplinary tactics, chores, and expectations will not be the same for all kids. Generally, though, I've seen that children are capable of doing much more than we ask them to do. Toddlers who have the manual dexterity to remove toys from a toy box also have the ability to put them back in, but are not usually motivated to do so. Four-year-olds are capable of many responsibilities, but often it's more trouble to cajole or train them to do a chore than to just do it ourselves.

This chapter looks at the typical stages of "misbehavior" kids evolve through, as well as age-appropriate behavioral responsibilities. General disciplinary techniques that work well for babies, toddlers, and young children are suggested by age group. Your child's personality will largely determine which techniques work best, and your personality and home situation will help guide you to select the techniques that you'll be most comfortable using.

For the child under three years of age, environmental engineering (child proofing) often helps her to stay out of trouble. In their book *Your One-Year-Old,* Louise Bates Ames and Frances L. Ilg note that a prime goal for the baby or toddler is "to just get through the day safely." However, they note that preverbal children become frustrated very easily because they have difficulty expressing their needs, and to further complicate matters, even if you have guessed correctly what they want, you may not choose to satisfy their desire at that moment (such as giving a cookie before dinner). The result: lots of frustration, leading to frequent temper tantrums and the need for some type of appropriate discipline.

Often the caretaker is more upset with the baby's or toddler's tantrum than is the child himself. Some kids are pros at turning the tears on and off like a faucet, but it's often difficult for the fretting parent to turn off the worry as easily.

For the baby and toddler, the most realistic disciplinary tactics are ignoring the behavior (looking the other way), distracting the child (handing him a toy while removing the forbidden object that he's playing with), changing the scenery (placing the frustrated seven-month-old in the playpen, or taking the fifteen-month-old for a quick ride in the car), or setting up the environment so that there's less for the toddler to get into. Environmental engineering not only means child proofing (ranging from using electrical outlet covers to putting away your prized crystal pieces for a few years), but also adapting a certain mind-set on your part. Assume that your child will spill at least a few hundred times before reaching kindergarten, then set up his eating area so that when the inevitable spill happens, you can take it in stride. Many families place baby's high chair on a piece of plastic covering the floor, making the mess easier to clean up. Assume that the wallpaper will be smeared with food at some point and either have a five-year plan to repaint or rewallpaper, or keep the high chair out of spitting or throwing distance.

Also try to look at the baby's environment from the child's point of view—and remember that whatever can happen most likely will! So, if you really don't want crayon or marker on your walls or drapes, keep these items stored high in a cabinet and bring them down only when you are available to supervise the activity.

The First Year

Misbehavior
Even young babies are capable of producing behaviors that may seem aggressive or irritating to the adult. You should not overreact, as these are generally exploratory behaviors. Extreme reactions on your part may actually reinforce the inappropriate behavior. T. Berry Brazelton, in his book *Touchpoints: Your Child's Emotional and Behavioral Development,* mentions the example of a four- or five-month-old who tries out her new teeth on her mother's nipple while nursing. Brazelton suggests taking firm action, not overreaction: "Every time the baby bites you, pull her firmly away but without too much overreaction; let the baby bite on your finger instead." As baby matures, her "misbehavior" may take the form of pulling or poking additional parts of your body. A firm "No" may get the point across. If not, restrain her hands and explain why you do not like being manhandled.

Behavioral Responsibilities
By three months of age, baby should be sleeping in his own crib, not in your bed. At six months, if he wakes up during the night, he should be able to calm himself down and need minimal parental attention in falling back to sleep. By nine months, your baby will begin trying finger foods, and may enjoy chopped-up hot dogs, Cheerios, carrot

sticks, and other veggies and fruits. At twelve months, your baby can learn to "help" put toys back in the playpen with your support (guide your baby with your hands, if necessary). Be sure to use lots of praise when a toy does make its way back in!

The Second Year

Misbehavior

Twelve- to fourteen-month-olds not only poke and pull, but they also add biting, pinching, and pushing others down to their list of behavioral crimes. Fifteen-month-olds tend to perform all of the above, but they now move on to new territory. They not only try out aggressive behavior on you, but also on the children they meet at day care, at the park, or while visiting your friends. The only problem is that, while you may react to a bite with a firm admonishment, another eighteen-month-old just might try to clean your child's clock. Either way, your kid will get the message that aggressive behavior will not be tolerated and perhaps is just not worth it.

Another common misbehavior during the second year is running away from you in public. I suggest using a child harness if your kid is a future world-class sprinter. If your son tends to climb out of the stroller or twists his hand out of your grasp while walking, the harness will keep him in reach and safe. Ignore the questioning looks you may receive from passersby; they are not responsible for your kid's safety and you need to keep him close to you.

Behavioral Responsibilities

At fifteen months of age, toddlers begin to respond to your verbal command of "No." Even if a fuss ensues, try not to give in and inadvertently reward the fussy toddler. By eighteen months, your child has the ability to respond to simple requests such as "Help put the blocks back in the box" or to come to you when called. By twenty-one months of age, try to insist on some verbalization before granting your child's requests, so that you don't have to play charades with a pointing child. At twenty-four months, you may want to test the waters in potty training; if there is no interest, drop it for a while and try again later. Begin to use a timer to motivate your child to clean up specific toys in a timely manner and to put them back in their proper place. Also, expect him to be able to sleep in his own bed at night with occasional waking up for comforting.

If the twelve- to twenty-four-month-old's tantrums are getting to you, try a minute of "in the corner" time-out for the child—or you may try putting *yourself* in a time-out situation! Consider soaking in the tub or taking a short walk around the block as long as there is another adult or responsible older child at home to supervise the toddler. If there's no one there to give you a hand and your nerves are frazzled, place the toddler in a safe playpen for a few minutes while you get a soda and regain your composure. I well remember my pediatrician's sage advice when I was a new mother with a crying baby: Sing a favorite song or put on the radio louder than the kid's crying. The situation can become quite humorous as you boogie around the kitchen, and often eases the aggravation of the moment. With little ones, remember that your goal may be as simple as getting through the day safely and accomplishing a few of the things you set out to do.

Remember, your child's priorities most likely are not even close to yours—you're lucky if you get anything accomplished. I'm convinced that's why grandparents and baby-sitters were invented—they're motivated to give you a break (they love to play with the grandkids or they appreciate the money earned while sitting). Even if funds are tight, paying a sitter or a day care center for a few hours will give you the break you need in order to come home and enjoy being with your child again, rather than just tolerating the situation. Mother's-day-out situations and sharing day care responsibilities with neighbors are inexpensive, or even free, ways to arrange some time for yourself.

The Third Year

Misbehavior

Although two-year-olds have more motor control than they did at an earlier age, they still have very little self-control. When frustrated, they tantrum and are not as easily distracted as they were when they were babies. One of the best tactics with this age group is to take advantage of the two-year-old's love of ritual. These kids enjoy structure and sameness, and, therefore, do not appreciate change in their daily routine. Try to set up rituals for the trouble spots during the day. Naptimes should directly follow lunch and toileting, and the bedtime ritual may include taking a bath, followed by listening to a book, kisses, and turning off the light. As repetition is important to the two-year-old, you may find the same book being requested over and over again, or the same outfit being desired three days in a row. It's not worth fighting your child on these issues—you don't want to win the battle and lose the war. Plenty of kids have grown up listening to *The Poky Little Puppy* for months on end, and it didn't stunt their intelligence one bit!

When you know that the child's environment will be changed, try to bring with you some sameness if possible. Be sure to take his favorite blanket or stuffed animal when you go on a car trip and try to stick to his favorite rituals as much as possible.

Two-year-olds almost always have different priorities than do their folks. Their number-one goal is to have fun, whereas most parents want to get things done. And the two sets of goals usually don't jibe. Be creative. Try to make the chores you're interested in accomplishing interesting for your child. I've seen many two-year-olds help out by playing beat the buzzer, throwing their toys back in the toy box before the timer goes off. Or sing your request to your child. Your two-year-old just may comply if you ask her to help out in a fun way.

Try not to set yourself up for a problem by directly asking your daughter if she'll do a task, without giving her any reward. Most likely the answer will be no, and then you're left either completing the task for her or getting into a face-off with the child. Instead, try to make the request fun, or tell her what nice thing will happen (a positive consequence) if she follows through with your request. If something really needs to be done quickly, avoid involving the child and just do it yourself. You'll find that you've saved yourself a lot of grief. Try to limit your requests for her help to situations when you are long on patience and time.

Behavioral Responsibilities

Between twenty-four and thirty-six months of age, your child develops the ability to handle many more behavioral responsibilities. Check again for interest in potty training. If your child seems motivated, give it a whirl. Also, use a timer to motivate your child to clean up specific toys and put them back in their proper place. It's also reasonable to expect your child to go to bed and stay in bed all night by this age.

Toward the end of the third year, expect your child to try different dinner foods and to decide on definite favorites. Kids this age also are able to respond to your firm "No" and cease disruptive behavior. Again, expect your child to verbally request and explain his needs and desires rather than just pointing to what he wants.

The Fourth Year

Misbehavior

By age three, children purposefully display anger outwardly by slamming doors, throwing toys as hard as they can, and, of course, temper tantrumming. Frustration tolerance is very difficult to develop and will continue to be throughout the youngster's childhood and perhaps adolescence.

By three years of age, your child will most likely be able to use a true behavior management program, such as the Smiley Face system I'll describe in chapter 6. She'll understand that "Smileys" are good and that having one crossed out is a negative event. So, by three years of age, you can move from the tactics used for one- and two-year-olds (distraction, ignoring, and change of scenery) to a true behavioral system involving Smiley Faces, time-outs, and rewards. Of course, never forget to heap on the praise and encouragement when your child is behaving well—a little bit of sugar always goes a long way toward encouraging appropriate behavior!

The flip side of praise and encouragement is scolding, and some kids respond well to stern admonishment. To others, it's like water off a duck's back. If that's your kid, it's probably best not to waste your words if they fall on deaf ears. Other families use spankings, and swear that even the threat of a swat gets their kids' attention. I believe that spankings should never be used as the main form of punishment. It is only one of many strategies that can be employed by the parent when necessary.

By three years of age, many kids are hooked on television and videos. These can provide excellent learning as well as entertainment experiences, as long as they are used wisely and not as a substitute for parental involvement. Television can also be employed as a privilege to be removed if misbehavior continues.

As with two-year-olds, three-year-olds love to play and have fun, and it is the wise parent who turns a chore into a game. Again, playing beat the buzzer often gets a kid into the tub, and using your child's imaginary friend ("Let's you and Mikey take a bath now") may be helpful in humoring a child into compliance.

Behavioral Responsibilities

Between three and four years of age, children are able to perform daily chores such as putting dirty clothes in a hamper (you may want to play beat the buzzer or dunk the basketball to get them moving on this) and helping you to make up the bed. Threes can fill pet bowls, pull up their own elastic-waist pants and skirts, as well as brush their teeth with your guidance.

The Fifth Year

Misbehavior

Four-year-olds like rules. They love to learn boundaries and limits, but also enjoy crossing over the line and breaking the rules. Thank goodness that most can be easily bribed into appropriate behavior, using food, privileges, and activities as rewards.

Fours are known for their silliness. Rhyming names and beginning potty language seem to be a rite of passage for the four-year-old. Sometimes simply ignoring this will discourage the child from continuing. If not, reprimands, losing Smileys on the Smiley Face system (see chapter 6), time-outs, or deprivation of privileges often does the trick in terms of getting your child back in line!

Many four-year-olds will also be experiencing preschool for the first time, and with new social and learning situations come new behavioral problems, notably social aggression and difficulty sharing. Try to stay on top of school issues by keeping in daily contact with the teacher either at drop-off or pickup times.

Behavioral Responsibilities

Four-year-olds continue to be able to complete chore responsibilities such as putting their dirty dishes on the counter or clothes in the hamper, giving the dog water, washing themselves in the bath with your supervision, brushing their teeth with your guidance, and picking out their clothes for the next day.

The Sixth and Seventh Years

Misbehavior

Five- and six-year-olds begin grade school, a wonderful and exciting addition to their lives, complete with meeting new friends, learning new skills, and dealing with complex social situations. Kindergarten and first grade also bring new pressures and responsibilities such as getting dressed on time, completing homework before going out to play, as well as getting to bed on time. These added pressures usually breed greater frustration, which often leads to an increase in temper tantrums. I've found that it's usually best to catch a tantrum as it's beginning. The loss of a Smiley Face or another appropriate negative consequence can tone down the fussing before it becomes a full-blown meltdown.

Fives and sixes can be very responsible kids, but only if their parents expect them to be. These kids also like to push limits, so expect lots of limit testing to occur and try to have a consequence in mind that will motivate them to behave. Negotiation, bribing, and bargaining usually work well with this age. Remember, though, don't try to win the battle only to lose the war. Pick the behavioral responsibilities wisely, but once chosen, try to stick to the expectations that are important to you and be consistent with the consequences.

Behavioral Responsibilities

Five-Year-Olds: Five-year-olds can prepare themselves for kindergarten in the morning and work fifteen minutes at a time on letters, dot-to-dots, and other preacademic tasks. Fives are able to share with siblings, can help make their own lunch, dress themselves, and begin to learn to tie their shoes. They can also help clean up after their bath (hanging up towels, putting dirty clothes in the hamper), as well as make their own bed.

Six-Year-Olds: Six-year-olds should be able to work on homework cooperatively with you. They can put their clean clothes in the correct drawers or hang them up in the closet, pick up their bedroom daily, and meet deadlines for bath- and bedtime. Sixes can be expected to brush their teeth by themselves and answer the telephone and respond politely when spoken to. They can help with dinner chores, take out their own articles from the car each day and put them away, come in from outside play when called, accept no for an answer, and still love to beat the buzzer when responding to adult requests.

Challenging Kids

When Parents Can't Say No

Day after day in my clinical practice, I see families with kids ranging in age from two through adolescence who are determined not to comply with parental requests. Often the kids are grumpy, whiny, or obnoxious—unconcerned with how their insensitive and selfish behaviors affect their families. Over the years, I've worked with so many families struggling to regain harmony that I've noticed an evolving pattern of misbehavior. And I'm not alone in this observation. Psychologists have had the opportunity for more than four decades to view a very disturbing trend in children's behavior. More and more kids appear to be lacking self-control, are egocentric, and display poor frustration tolerance. This is disturbing because learning to delay gratification and to accept that at times the world may be unfair helps to prepare kids for the frustrating events that inevitably will crop up throughout their lives. Many parents are not teaching these skills, and their children will be the ones to pay.

Why are parents today so conflicted about setting limits and using discipline? I believe that it's based in ineffective parental training. Over the past forty years, many psychologists, pediatricians, and child care workers have taught parents to view conflicts with their children merely as differences of opinion and misunderstandings. These child-rearing experts have proposed that using discipline to teach may even be harmful, and therefore reasoning, understanding, and discussing have become the mainstays of discipline. This laissez-faire attitude asks parents to allow "natural consequences" to affect their children. In her book *Reviving Ophelia: Saving the Selves of Adolescent Girls,* Mary Pipher suggests that some folks confuse *parenting* with *abuse*, that saying no to a child may be harmful. In effect, parents have been taught to try to "reason with the unreasonable," but young children tend to be egocentric and normally have not yet developed the ability to see things from others' perspectives.

In the classic book *Dare to Discipline,* James Dobson reports that parents have been taught that a child "will eventually respond to patience and tolerance, ruling out the need for discipline. . . . Parents have been told to encourage the child's rebellion because it offered a valuable release of hostility." According to Dobson, some experts recommend that parents should verbalize or reflect the child's feelings when she is upset, such as saying, "You want the water, but you're angry because I brought it too late," as the child is dumping the glass on the ground. But emotional reflection does little to teach the youngster better behavior and may actually promote poor frustration tolerance.

In this atmosphere of disciplinary uncertainty, is it any wonder that parents today are confused? In *Touchpoints: Your Child's Emotional and Behavioral Development,* Dr. T. Berry Brazelton notes that "when both parents are away at work all day, they hate to be disciplinarians in their limited time at home. But children will save their provocative behavior all day to try it out in a safe, loving environment." Not wanting to discipline their kids because of guilt feelings or fear of conflict, many folks then simply disengage themselves from the parenting role. But sooner or later, these parents may begin to feel as if they are being held hostage by their own children.

It's interesting that toasters, CD players, and Lego sets come with complex instructions in at least two languages, but our most precious new acquisition, a baby, does not. We go to Lamaze class for pain preparation and consult an interior decorator for designing baby's room, yet how many prospective parents actively put even one-tenth of their prebaby time and budget into learning about child care and development? We spend hours poring over baby name books, agonizing between the psychological effects of naming our son Michael versus Jason, but allow little to no time discussing some disciplinary tactics. Parents have specific ideas about how they want their children to *be*—motivated in school, respectful to adults, sensitive and caring—but they often do not focus on the day-to-day specifics of their child's behavior until they find that one day Junior has taken over the family.

The Consequence of No Consequences

Childhood is the training ground for later adult behavior. The lessons parents teach their children, both purposefully and inadvertently, are long-lasting and color their children's future adult actions and temperament. It is the parents' job to teach the child. Kids will change their behaviors when their parents change their expectations. If a parent expects a child to develop good self-control, the child will do so if the stage is set from an early age.

Children with adequate self-control will develop into adults who are self-disciplined and productive. It is the exceptional young adult who has led a chaotic adolescence with little parental guidance and then "sees the light" as an adult, finishes high school and college, and becomes successful. Sure, there are individuals among us like that. However, the majority of these kids evolve into irresponsible adults, because these seeds were planted in their early years.

In *The Road Less Traveled: A New Psychology of Love, Traditional Values and Spiritual Growth,* Dr. M. Scott Peck notes that "discipline is the basic set of tools we require to solve life's problems. Without discipline we can solve nothing, and with some discipline we can solve only some problems. With total discipline we can solve all problems." Youngsters who were taught self-control at an early age often were exposed to disciplinary tactics by their parents as a natural part of the developmental process. These kids develop and understand self-discipline naturally as adults. Most likely, they will also pass this gift on to their own kids, perpetuating a positive approach to disciplining children.

But when parents are themselves undisciplined and therefore offer poor role models for their children, the tools for the development of self-control are not passed on to the next generation, and irresponsible values and impulsivity are transferred from parent to child. This impulsive, irresponsible lifestyle will follow the children into and through adulthood. Breaking the cycle of low frustration tolerance, irresponsibility, and self-indulgence is a must if the next generation is to succeed.

Parents cannot look to educators, ministers, or pediatricians to teach their children responsibility and self-discipline. It must come from the home environment. Consistent, strong, well-disciplined parents are the prescription for the evolution of self-disciplined, successful youngsters. Families in which children are in charge are chaotic, unpleasant environments for *all*—parents, kids, relatives, friends, neighbors, and even complete strangers who end up drawn into a family drama. Kids are happier and more self-confident when they know the rules and realize that they can live within the guidelines.

How Parents Lose Control

It is interesting how kids come to control a family. Most parents have very good intentions. They give *unconditional love*, meaning, "I will continue to love you no matter what you do," but many also engage in *unconditional giving*. They love their children and will give them everything they can. They give in the material sense and in terms of time and attention. The process seems to go awry, however, when the parent gives to the child *unconditionally*. Parents tend to reward youngsters inadvertently for very inappropriate behaviors.

For example, the four-year-old who continues to bug his folks to buy him a treat in the grocery store is all too typical. His father may have said no twice, then Junior begins to pitch a fit and Mom lets him open the cereal box and dig in just to quiet him down. In this case, the unconditional reward (eating the treat) only serves to teach him the inappropriate lesson that harassing and manipulating achieves one's goals.

Caring parents often *want* to give children unconditional rewards—whatever they can afford to give. In addition, unconditional rewards are often used in an effort to avoid conflict. Most parents do not enjoy getting into arguments with their kids and tend to take the easy way out. This usually means giving in to the child, which results in gaining the immediate goal. It is obvious, however, that unconditional rewards are not in the youngster's long-term best interest. The real world will not often give in to temper tantrums and demanding behavior.

Thus the child may grow up without learning appropriate tactics to deal with frustration. Youngsters who do not learn how to take no for an answer tend to become adolescents who are impulsive and irresponsible. Instead of attending a boring class, impulsive kids tend to skip school to do something that is more fun. All too often they end up in juvenile court being lectured by a judge about responsibility. It's nearly impossible for them to stay at a job because a promotion may be years away, or to learn new behaviors in order to save a marriage. These kids are often later seen as individuals with unstable work patterns and marital problems.

As parents, we tend to avoid dealing with conflict because our kids often make us feel guilty when things do not go their way. We ask ourselves, "What would our parents have done in this situation?" or "What will the effect be on my child if I do not allow him to have what he is asking for or to do what he wants to do?" In an effort to do the best job that we can, parents often give their children too much. *Too much* includes too many material objects, too many freedoms, and too much control over others. In the process of giving our kids too much, parents are not teaching them enough of a very important skill—that of self-control. The issues of self-control, responsibility, and frustration tolerance are integral parts of an effective child-rearing program.

Parenting Myths

As well as losing control in their families, parents often have difficulty dealing with the different personality styles of their children. Sometimes one kid is easier to get along with while another is tough to warm up to, or a parent may feel that she has not "bonded" appropriately with her child—all this adds up to a good case of the guilts. Myth has it that kids and their folks should instantly bond and enjoy each other—but that's not always the case.

I met Don and Allison at a New Year's Eve party last year and the topic soon turned to New Year's resolutions. My husband and I announced the typical "lose weight, get in shape" proclamation that has become a thirty-day standard in our family. We're great for about three or four weeks and then tend to let time pressures, travel, and mainly food take over.

Don and Allison, though, had an unusual resolution, one that I had never heard before as a New Year's request. They were determined to understand their five-year-old daughter's personality, to foster her becoming more like her brother in order to "fit" better within the family. Caitlin, who was a twin to Jason, was definitely her own person. Although she looked like her mother, she neither acted nor thought like either parent or Jason. Don noted that Jason was compliant by nature, took minor disappointments in stride, and responded well to the few punishments he had received over the years. Jason appeared to understand the need for command decisions made by his folks, and although he may have disagreed with the decision, he rarely fought it. Allison felt that for his age Jason was quite reasonable and was a joy to raise.

Caitlin, on the other hand, was an enigma. Allison swore that if she hadn't seen her being born, she would have questioned whether her baby had been switched at birth. This kid popped out with a mind of her own. She was the loudest and fussiest baby in the nursery, and, even as a newborn, nothing seemed to satisfy her. Her parents tried changing from breast milk to formula to soy, hoping that simple food allergies were the culprit. After six futile months of experimenting with different foods, sleeping arrangements, fabric softeners, and holding positions, Allison and Don found themselves at the pediatrician's office at their wits' end.

The doctor, who had been around the block a few times, concluded that Caitlin was indeed their child, and although she had inherited her mother's looks, she had inherited neither of her parents' temperaments. Caitlin's philosophy was "my way or the highway"—pity the unsuspecting person who tried to get in her way! Caitlin's parents realized that they needed to find a way to get along with and work with their daughter in a better manner.

I was fascinated by the story, and we moved to a quiet place in the living room to continue talking after dinner. I learned that Caitlin's folks had gone through various stages of acceptance, similar to those people go through after a death or loss. Confusion as to how to deal with an extremely stubborn, egocentric child led to a flurry of blaming themselves as well as others for her behavior. Intermittent periods of hope popped up when Caitlin appeared to be coming around, but these times inevitably resulted in a letdown as her somewhat selfish nature came through. Allison and Don blamed each other and felt guilty about their mixed emotions toward Caitlin, especially in light of their warm relationship with Jason. They confided that their feelings were turning toward disappointment and anger when they blamed Caitlin for her behavior, or toward guilt when they felt that she was like this because of something they had or had not done while raising her. What had them stymied, though, was that they felt they had brought up both kids in basically the same atmosphere. Jason had even shared the womb with Caitlin, and yet displayed a significantly different personality!

After listening to their heartbreaking yet all too common story, I proposed that they do some reading on two concepts basic to developmental psychology—the "nature/nurture controversy" and the concept of "goodness of fit."

"Nature/Nurture"

Let's take a look at "nature/nurture" first. Nature means genetics—physical aspects such as hair and eye coloring, shape of nose, height, bone structure, and weight. These characteristics are easily seen and usually can be traced back to the owner—Dad's blue eyes or Mom's auburn hair.

Genetically based personality traits are more difficult to describe and even harder to trace back to the predecessor. Just as Junior may have inherited hazel eyes from the combined genes of his blue-eyed mother and green-eyed father, his temperament may be a combination of both their natures, or it may resemble one parent more strongly than the other.

Genetic traits and predispositions to traits (the latter not necessarily seen at a young age but emerging later when sparked by environmental influence) have been studied for decades by scientists of all persuasions. Psychological researchers tend to focus upon genetically based personality variables, and have found that very young infants can be divided into distinct categories of temperament.

Jerome Kagan has spent years observing and documenting this phenomenon, and has found through longitudinal studies that, indeed, child temperament is largely inborn and that it is fairly stable and permanent. Timid babies are more withdrawn and wary than uninhibited ones and remain so for many years. Alexander Thomas and Stella Chess have come to similar conclusions. Their research suggests that about 10 percent of newborns are "difficult" babies—they cry frequently, are prone to tantrums, and are hard to pacify. "Slow to warm up" babies (about 15 percent) have low activity levels, seem to be withdrawn, and are wary in new situations. "Easy" babies (about 40 percent) are cheerful and quickly adapt to new situations. The remaining 35 percent show a mixture of traits that do not fit easily into these categories.

That's the nature side of the argument. What about nurture or environmental influence? I've come to accept that genetics sets the blueprint for the way children view the world. Whether the youngster will be a risk taker and jump off his roof just to see what it feels like to fly or whether he'll be the one on the ground cheerfully (and safely) congratulating the would-be aviator is based largely in the genetic blueprint. As in Don and Allison's case, both kids were raised with the same expectations, yet Caitlin's genetic blueprint—her temperamental wiring, so to speak—was different from her brother's, and so was her behavior.

In cases in which children differ greatly in nature, I've come to the conclusion that it's best to celebrate their individual strengths while attempting to modify the behaviors that are less attractive. Caitlin's selfish behavior should be brought to her attention and definitely not catered to because that will only increase its frequency. She should receive a negative consequence for pitching a fit when her needs are not met and be praised when she does decide to go along with the flow. In this way, nurture (environmental factors) will modify nature as much as possible.

It's a daunting and often frustrating task to try to change anyone's temperament—yours, your partner's, or your children's. It's easier with kids than with adults, I'm convinced, because parents have more control over the things that children want—motivators such as money (for toys), control of the refrigerator (for food treats), and, later on, the car keys (to go to neat places). In counseling lots of families with kids whose temperaments drive their folks wild, I've found that consistent usage of these motivators can change some of the inappropriate behaviors of children whose nature dictates egocentricity or selfishness. The new behaviors will conform more to your liking—and hopefully the attitude that is at the root of the offensive behaviors will change also. It's worth a shot, and if you, the parent, don't try to teach the ornery, egocentric child how to share, to develop frustration tolerance, and at least to act as if she can see things from others' viewpoints, who will? Most kids I've worked with using this philosophy do come around, but perhaps not until their teen years. That might not be very soothing to the parent of a hard-to-please two-year-old, but it sure beats the alternative—raising a child who has never learned how to develop self-control or to curb egocentricity.

"Goodness of Fit"

Let's talk about a parenting myth that's seldom spoken of, but that has caused endless guilt in many families—that of "goodness of fit." Somewhere, folklore has it that parents should bond with their newborns in the first day or two. But there are really two times for bonding—when the baby is a newborn, and around the baby's first birthday.

Let's look at the newborn issue first. People "bond" (form a deep emotional attachment) to their babies at different rates. Some fall in love with the child while he's still in the womb and others when they hear the first wail in the delivery room. Still other parents need time and exposure with their little one before they truly believe that he's theirs to keep. Realizing the enormous responsibility for another life often triggers the bonding experience as the parents understand that their baby literally cannot survive without their constant care and supervision. Feeling needed is a huge boost to the bonding process, and it is not necessarily instantaneous. So don't get hung up on bonding—it will come as you and baby get to know each other.

The second stage of bonding often emerges around the child's first birthday, when she's had a good long gawk at your personality and you at hers. If you are both pleased with what you see, then most likely you and your child will have developed what psychologists refer to as appropriate "goodness of fit." This occurs when the youngster's temperamental nature jibes with yours, or perhaps is different but in a way that you respect. When there is "goodness of fit," relationships are often easy and rewarding to both parent and child. Getting along with each other is a breeze, as both parties are on the same wavelength and rarely cross each other.

"Goodness of fit" is common in most families. "Fit" is based in both nature and nurture, and therefore the odds are that parents have produced children whose genetic dispositions are similar in many ways to their own. In addition, they most likely have set up environmental demands that go along with their own natures, so that the children are automatically taught what the parents believe to be important.

The fly in the ointment occurs when a baby is born "wired" differently from his folks. I've seen many of these kids over the years. A common example is the hyperactive little scamp whose parents are mellow and laid back. This type of kid can keep even an active parent on her toes, but what he does to a laid-back, slow-burner parent is not pretty. What can be more upsetting to the family relationship is the mellow mom married to the hyper father who relishes his son's energy level. Mom often feels frustrated and that she doesn't belong,

Dad doesn't understand why she can't see the humor in Junior's antics, and the child is just plain confused.

Or how about the opposite scenario? I've met many folks who grew up involved in every activity available, still playing golf and tennis as adults and participating in local community activities. Their daughter, however, is a couch potato who sees absolutely no reason to waste her energy on something as silly as movement.

These folks have a problem—a lack of "goodness of fit." And, I believe, there is no real cure for it—only learning to take a different perspective. First, try to respect each other's personality and style of temperament—yours may be different from your child's but not necessarily better or worse. Next, attempt to find or develop something in common. If you absolutely despise sports but your active six-year-old loves them, go to his games, but bring a good book to read when he's not at bat. And try not to take his behavior too seriously. If he seems to favor his father, who may enjoy similar interests, keep this in perspective. Your son does not love you any less than he does his dad; he just may enjoy his father's company more, and probably with good reason. Search for areas that can become special between you and your child so that he'll be reassured that you love, like, and respect him. Julie Davis, writing in *Child* magazine, summarizes this point: "Temperaments can be modified by parents' response. Parents have to realize that they're not necessarily going to get the type of kid they want. It's a matter of changing some of their own expectations."

PARENTING STYLES: WHY WE PARENT THE WAY WE DO

Every one of us was raised by an authority figure of some sort—birth parent, stepparent, adoptive parent, foster parent, orphanage, or grandmother—so we all have had the opportunity to come into contact with at least one parenting style. Parents differ tremendously in disciplinary tactics. Some are militaristic and others laissez-faire, while some flip-flop between the two depending upon how things went at the office that day.

I've found that the least effective parenting style is the parent who is *consistently inconsistent*—changing tactics, demands, and consequences to meet his or her own immediate needs and moods. These parents tend to confuse their kids, leading to frightened children who must constantly tread on thin ice around their folks, and to manipulative kids who use guilt tactics to avoid any consequences for their own behavior.

How do parents develop their individual disciplinary styles? Many, I'm convinced, don't think ahead, they just fall into whatever seems to work at the moment. They use a mixture of one part talk-show-guru suggestion, two parts mother and mother-in-law input, and a bit of what the nosy neighbor next door throws in. Of course their child is a mess. Who wouldn't be when there is no well-thought-out disciplinary plan?

I believe that new parents don't talk to each other about discipline early on because they feel that it won't come into play before the child's second birthday. Are they ever wrong! Discipline needs to start in the baby's first few months of life, when structure should become a part of the daily routine in the form of naps, feeding, and bedtime.

Parents also tend to make decisions about discipline, consequences, and consistency based upon their own childhood experiences. If your folks were militaristic and it worked, you might try the same tactics. If you grew up resenting that strictness and fell into a rebellious stage, you probably will try the opposite tack. Often, we swing 180 degrees from our childhood experience. The bitter child of militaristic parents becomes a wishy-washy father. The wandering child of laissez-faire folks may parent like Attila the Hun, often overreacting and enforcing rules that are just not necessary.

You'll know that your disciplinary tactics are off-base by watching your kids' reactions to them. If your children show you a lack of respect, you're probably tolerating too much inappropriate behavior. If, on the other hand, they appear to be fearful of you, then you're probably too strict. These are red flags suggesting that you have overdone a parenting tactic. Try a more compromising approach, one that meets your needs as a parent as well as your child's.

Look at your own family situation. Are your kids pretty reasonable? Do they listen well? Does your spouse back you up when you've made a command decision? If the answer is yes, then perhaps your family will thrive on a middle-of-the-road approach—important rules prevail, but let the little stuff go and give a warning instead of an immediate consequence for infractions. But if your kids are becoming discipline problems, you need to step back and analyze your parenting style.

The Cardinal Rules for Parenting

I will discuss the various parenting styles in this chapter and later present what style I feel to be the most effective in certain situations. But regardless of the parenting style you use, there are two cardinal rules for disciplining kids:

1. Be consistent (this can't be said enough).
2. Take a cool, calm, and almost nonchalant attitude when giving

out consequences. A screaming, red-faced parent is often quite amusing to a kid.

Although they won't admit it, kids want limits, because limits in the home often provide the only security that children experience. Kids need predictability—they need to know what's going to happen next, what positive consequences will occur if they work hard, and what discomfort they will have to endure if they slack off. Parents who are on opposite ends of the spectrum—either overpermissive or irrationally strict—cause children to guess at the consequences of their behavior.

And don't forget the calm, nonchalant attitude mentioned above as a cardinal rule. Even the best consequence can be ineffectual if the parent falls into a screaming meltdown! When Mom and Dad speak in a firm yet calm tone of voice, rather than yelling, kids tend to take them seriously.

To state it simply, consequences need to be immediate, important to the child, predictable, and calmly given. Rules that lead to consequences should be clear, jointly determined by both parent and child, and fair. So, if you find yourself constantly reasoning, cajoling, nagging, yelling, and reminding your child to complete tasks or decrease a certain obnoxious behavior, quit beating a dead horse and learn some new tactics. It's time for action, and your child *will* respond.

Quiz Time

I bet some of you are wondering whether you need to change your parenting style. Well, it's time for a short quiz. Be honest when answering these questions. You'll know that you are trying to "reason with the unreasonable" instead of disciplining your child appropriately if you answer yes to most of the following items.

1. You wonder why you can't just be your child's friend (buddy, chum) and not have to force him to do things he doesn't want to do.

2. You flash back to how you were raised, and the word "disci-

pline" sends chills down your spine. You vowed to give your kids negative consequences only as a last resort, if ever.

3. You argue constantly with your spouse, who wants to give your son time-out in the corner for not putting away his toys when told. You feel there is nothing wrong with having to constantly remind your son to clean up his toys because, well, "Boys will be boys."

4. You've never really been strict and consistent in your own life—and the thought of setting up rules and actually having to follow through with them is very frightening. You're more worried about your own failure to use a system of rules than about your child's ability to succeed.

5. You've tried everything—time-out, taking away privileges, spankings—and nothing seems to work.

6. You suffer more than your child does when she is in time-out. You feel guilty when she gets upset as she is punished.

7. You're afraid your child will hate you if you make him lose out on a privilege. You believe this feeling toward you will be permanent.

8. Your spouse overreacts and punishes too quickly, so you feel that you must play the "buffer" and be lenient with your child. This way your kid experiences either leniency or abuse but rarely a compromised, reasonable position.

9. You feel frustrated and powerless after discussing an inappropriate behavior with your kid for the umpteenth time, but he seems so sincere, and those big eyes make you melt and give in.

10. You want to leave. Who asked for these darned kids to begin with?

If you admit to many of these feelings and behaviors, you're probably not parenting as effectively as you could. You may find yourself to be a "happiness-seeking" parent, a "wait-'til-your-father-gets-home" parent, an uninvolved parent, or one who is in denial of your kid's inappropriate behavior.

The Happiness-Seeking Parent

Happiness-seeking parents' primary purpose is to make their child as happy as possible. I've learned, however, that the best way to ensure that your daughter will be miserable and unhappy as an adult is for you to focus totally on her happiness as a child. Sound a little nutty? What else would you want for your kid except her happiness? After years of experience, I have come to realize that parents who try to make their children happy are not only spinning their wheels, they are actually interfering with their child's healthy development.

How does the pursuit of kid happiness mess up your child? First, no one (not even you) can make your youngster happy. Comfort, pleasure, and good self-esteem are the roots of happiness and contentment, and no one can artificially inject these qualities into another human being. Yet, no matter how much you give to your son, love him, and shower him with things, self-content can still be elusive. Happiness is based in how your child feels about himself and how others feel about him, realizing that he is a good person, and developing self-control so that he can tolerate the frustrating situations that will inevitably crop up in his life as he grows and matures.

I see only kids and their folks in my clinical practice, and almost daily I encounter the happiness-seeking syndrome: "My kid is going to be happy at any cost and *I* am responsible for his happiness." Ten years ago, happiness seekers tended to be yuppies who were determined not to make a single mistake raising their children. However, it seems that this trend has generalized to parents of every socioeconomic status—almost as a disease spreads insidiously. These parents read magazines, watch news coverage, and are glued to talk shows that focus on the "negative adult remnants of early childhood parenting mistakes." The media have made them afraid to parent their own kids.

Typical of the happiness seekers are my clients Judy and Michael and their kids, three-and-one-half-year-old Marissa and five-year-old Mikey. Since both parents work outside the home, they continually worry whether they are giving enough time and attention to their two children. Judy and Michael are very proud of their kids. Mikey is already showing signs of becoming quite an athlete and Marissa is a budding computer whiz even at her young age. The parents marvel at how quickly their children catch on to new ideas and activities that they enjoy. But both seem to have difficulty accepting parental requests as well as responsibilities. And Judy and Michael do not ask much of their kids, partially because they feel that as preschoolers not much should be asked of them, but mostly because the kids start whining and become obnoxious when they are forced to do anything that they don't want to do. In order to avoid the fuss, the parents usually give in and let the kids get away with the misbehavior.

Both Judy and Michael have reasons why they are so intent upon keeping the children as happy as possible. Michael's folks had divorced when he was in grade school, and since then, his family's financial situation had been tough. His mother couldn't afford to buy extras, and as the oldest of three boys, Michael was responsible for many chores as he was growing up, which he resented. He was determined that his kids would not have to be so burdened or to endure so many disappointments. Therefore, he chose to do everything in his power to *make* them happy and carefree. Mikey and Marissa were showered with toys and games and had free rein of the television and Nintendo sets, and were frequently taken to their favorite fun spots.

Judy had a different experience growing up. Although her folks remained married, they fought constantly. Because her mother had such difficulty with her father, Judy's mom used her as a confidante and actually treated her as a buddy. Because Judy became her mother's equal, she was rarely disciplined by her. Dad tended to try to "buy" her affection in an effort to remain close to at least one of the women in his life.

Naturally, Judy modeled her parents' parenting styles (Mom's chumlike philosophy and Dad's avoidance of discipline) and, like Michael, did whatever she felt was necessary to keep the kids content, even if it meant putting up with some pretty bratty behavior.

The problem was that at three and one-half and five years of age, Marissa and Mikey didn't appear to be content. They were whiny, had a very low tolerance for frustration, and never seemed quite satisfied. If one received a new toy for a birthday, the other pitched a fit. Their folks, therefore, soon started the ritual of buying *both* kids gifts for each other's birthdays. It just wasn't worth the hassle to put up with the fuss and to watch the birthday child's sibling have to deal with frustration.

In therapy, I counseled Judy and Michael to give their kids adequate time and attention, but to teach Marissa and Mikey to earn their toys and privileges. No more receiving treats at the grocery store just for going with Mom, they now had to behave appropriately in order to get a cookie before going through the checkout line.

These parents were taught that a little bit of indulgence can be a good thing, but it's generally quite harmful for a child to be raised on a steady diet of "me as the center of the universe." Why? Because Mikey and Marissa are not the center of the universe and never will be. Better their parents prepare them for the reality of having to share and, yes, even to experience disappointment and unhappiness. This is not to say that unhappy events should be promoted and planned by parents, but rather that children should not be protected from everyday disappointments. Unpleasantness, peer rejection, and self-consciousness are part of the stuff of growing up, and kids who are sheltered from the realities of childhood as well as the responsibilities of maturation often grow up to be bitter, irresponsible adults who never quite adjust to society's demands. Children who are raised with a feeling of entitlement become easily depressed as teenagers and adults when their peers refuse to cater to their whims. Adult temper tantrums are scorned by others, and Mom and Dad can no longer make the world a rosy place.

I believe that it was much harder for Judy and Michael to change their behavior than for the kids to adjust to the new rules. They occasionally still felt guilty when saying no to their kids, and old tapes of their own childhoods still ran through their minds. However, Mikey and Marissa quickly responded better to their parents' requests once their immediate happiness was not the focus of Judy and Michael's lives. The kids' behavior and character became the barometer of success.

I'm not suggesting that this type of change is easy. Changing parenting styles can be quite tough. In fact, it can be downright awful! But even more disheartening is the realization later in your child's life that your adorable, overindulged little one has grown into a selfish, insecure, and unprepared adult. Do not focus on winning the battle (immediate kid satisfaction) while losing the war (adult happiness and self-respect). Children who are catered to often become so egocentric that they cannot place themselves in others' shoes and are, therefore, often labeled as insensitive and selfish. Peers soon learn to avoid them, considering the child a nuisance or an irritant. Surely not the recipe for happiness that the parents of the indulged child planned for!

Happiness is a by-product of good parenting. You cannot buy it, fake it, talk your child into it, or manipulate the world to provide it. Happiness is a state of comfort that develops when you are content with your relationships with others, having developed a healthy balance between fulfilling your own needs while helping others with theirs. Happy kids are secure in the knowledge that they can control their emotions and behavior so that no matter what challenges they face, they can act appropriately. Spoiled, entitled children rarely rise to this level of character, and they forever pay for their parents' indulgence.

Think about it—it's never too soon to start setting limits, to say no to unreasonable requests, and to begin to build your child's character in a healthy way. In his provocative book *Emotional Intelligence*, Daniel Goleman provides statistics from several studies showing that parents who are involved and who set consistent guidelines for their children are rewarded with young adults who have developed "a set of traits—some call it character—that also matter immensely for our personal destiny." As well, studies show that most people who develop good character also enjoy positive self-esteem, are well liked by others, and yes, *turn out to be very happy*.

Quiz Time

Happiness seeking is an easy trap to fall into, but one that you can avoid by better understanding your feelings and motivations as a parent. Check it out in your home. If you see yourself in the following items, you may be a happiness-seeking parent.

1. You give in to your child because you can't bear to see her unhappy (sad, miserable, hurting).

2. You distort the truth so that your kid feels good about herself at the expense of not realizing her shortcomings. ("Johanna doesn't want to play with you anymore because there is something wrong with Johanna . . . you didn't do anything wrong.")

3. You are unable to criticize your youngster because you fear you will damage his self-esteem, even at the cost of not helping him to correct character flaws that will cause him problems later in his life.

4. You rush to fulfill your child's every wish because he is sad, mad, or unhappy, and you become upset when he is frustrated.

5. You feel guilty or that you are a bad or ineffective parent when your child doesn't agree with your decisions.

6. You feel that you, as the parent, have the power, ability, and responsibility to cure your kid's peer arguments and friend problems.

7. You dread your child's moodiness when she doesn't get her way. You avoid saying no to her because you just don't want to deal with the fallout.

8. You often walk on eggshells around your kids.

9. You generally put your needs after your child's whims—even if he doesn't seem to notice or appreciate what you do for him.

10. You were not a happy child, and you vowed never to let upsetting things happen to your kids.

The Wait-'Til-Your-Father-Gets-Home Parent

The wait-'til-your-father-gets-home parent is another frequent visitor to my office. This style is actually a double dose of bad parenting. First, the *waiting* part is precarious because discipline should occur as soon as possible after the infraction, and, second, parents need to present a united front when doling out the consequences for inappropriate behavior.

Although I've seen some wait-'til-your-mother-gets-home situations, most kids I've worked with tend to take their fathers more seriously than their moms. Surprisingly, many kids who respond better to their fathers than to their mothers do not report doing so because Dad spanks harder than Mom—in fact, most of these families do not use corporal punishment. They say it's the deeper voice, or Dad's larger size, but it's a fairly consistent pattern.

Many families go through a period of time without Dad being a constant presence. This may be due to his long working hours, a job that involves traveling weekdays and being home only on weekends, or periods of separation or even divorce between the parents. My clients Sharon and David were experiencing such a disruptive situation. David was the field representative for a carpet-manufacturing company and frequently spent three or four days a week driving from city to city, touching base with his clients. He kept a hectic schedule, but did a good job checking in with Sharon each night to see how she and their two children were faring. David's previous position allowed him to work for the manufacturer from his home, taking orders and fielding customer complaints. However, that job had been phased out and David had to take the traveling position in order not to lose his job with the company. He didn't relish being without his wife and kids several days a week, especially since he had been the main disciplinarian while he was working out of the home.

Sharon especially disliked David's new job, as she had to take on the responsibility for disciplining her four- and six-year-old daughters, and she felt uncomfortable having to set limits for them. Sharon's nature was somewhat of a "marshmallow mom," tending to give in when her daughters begged for extra treats or privileges, because she didn't want to disappoint them. She yearned for David's presence when the kids were especially demanding and she felt that they were out of control. Sharon noted to me at one of our sessions that she actually felt helpless in dealing with discipline, not knowing what to do when the kids began arguing or begging for a special privilege.

David, on the other hand, felt that Sharon was "passing the buck" by waiting for his nightly phone calls home in order for him to discipline the children, often being asked to deal with infractions that occurred much earlier in the day. David let Sharon know that he felt she was acting irresponsibly and that her helpless behavior around the kids was inappropriate.

In therapy, I described to David how Sharon's nature was to be compliant and to avoid conflict at any cost, and that was how she'd gotten into the situation of using the "wait-'til-your-father-gets-home" tactic. David, on the other hand, was an "in-charge" type of person, and he felt comfortable setting limits for the girls.

I suggested that the family set up a behavior management program to help Sharon develop various consequences to use for infractions as they occurred. This had to be developed gradually, as Sharon would have difficulty in establishing and maintaining strict limits and rules. Over the weeks, though, Sharon was able to become more consistent in using behavior management by setting limits, telling the girls no and sticking to her guns, as well as giving negative and positive consequences for their behavior.

David was especially thankful for the changes Sharon was making, as his nightly telephone calls home became pleasant interactions with his wife and kids, not just listening to a laundry list of crimes committed. Although both parents wished that David could return home and work out of the house again, they knew that they had developed a behavioral program that Sharon could live with until David could find a job more compatible with his family's needs. In the meantime, though, Sharon had learned to expect respect from her children, and she actually felt better about herself as a person through this process.

The message I give to wait-'til-your-father-gets-home parents is that your kid needs to learn to respect *you* and to comply with *your* wishes. Children who have a bit of healthy fear of their parents tend to be good kids. Many folks think I'm a few screws short when I suggest that a child who fears his parents is a healthy child. What I mean by healthy fear is the child thinking, "If I don't do what Mom wants me to do I'll lose out on something—such as not watching cartoons or getting to go outside to play. Maybe I should listen to her because that would really be boring!"

That's what I mean by setting up healthy fear. It's definitely not fear of being physically or emotionally hurt by a parent. It's your child's realistic concern that you, as a parent, will actually give negative consequences for negative behaviors. Pretty scary thought for a kid, and it really works if you've been consistent and have set up a plan of action. Even if you're only 80 percent consistent, your kid will become a believer.

Healthy fear leads to healthy respect. I see it happen all the time in my practice. Try an experiment. Ask your friends, "When you were growing up, who was the heavy in your family?" Many will say it was their father. And if he used healthy consequences (not beatings, cursing, or ridiculous punishments), most of your friends will add that they listened to him, either because they respected him or because they didn't want to find out what would happen if they didn't follow Dad's requests. Many probably will report that they also respected their mothers—again, because Mom (perhaps in a gentler way) stood her ground, and they knew that if they ever wanted to be released from grounding or restrictions, then they had better mind their manners.

Another group will note that they loved their mother but didn't particularly respect her, and also felt sorry for Mom because she couldn't seem to control the kids. Or that they feared their father, and rather than respecting him, actually hated him. These types of families were those in which the wait-'til-your-father-gets-home threat was liberally used. Mom was not taken seriously, and Dad was feared because when he did get home, inappropriate and often harsh consequences were given. Kids were spanked or yelled at for their misbehavior. This type of situation does not foster respect; it evolves into pity and disrespect for Mom (and still little child compliance, by the way) and hatred for Dad.

And it's not fair to either parent. Mom feels that her hands are tied, and Dad feels used. He's so busy punishing that it's almost impossible for him to develop a good relationship with his children. And, after a while, these patterns become so ingrained that these disciplinary tactics actually become bad habits, behaviors used even though they are ineffective.

Why do folks become victim to this parenting style? Partly because kids can drive you so nuts that if you don't have a reasonable behavior management system ready to use at your fingertips, you just react. Passive parents become hostages to their tyrannical kids, and aggressive parents bypass reasonable compromises and leap to intimidation and abuse. Neither of these styles leads to respect. The kids end up pitying or ignoring the weak parent and feeling a great deal of bitterness and resentment toward the frightening one.

If this scenario sounds all too familiar to you, why not just stop the cycle right now? Commit to making some changes, such as using a behavior management system of rules and limit setting. Kids who are about 80 percent sure of the consequences of their actions—because no parent is 100 percent consistent all the time—respect their parents, even if it means disliking the consequence.

A small amount of healthy fear of an appropriate, humane, and predictable consequence goes a long way. And, as a bonus, when Dad doesn't have to come home to a disastrous situation that he must handle, he'll tend to be calmer and more pleasant, and he'll actually have the opportunity to develop good relationships with his kids. I realize that often it's easier to continue with an ineffective old pattern rather than to try a potentially successful new behavior. New things tend to frighten us, and fear is something we like to avoid. However, there are big stakes at risk here, folks, and I think the payoff is worth the risk.

Quiz Time
You're falling into the wait-'til-your-father-gets-home trap if:
1. You literally use that phrase at least three times a week.
2. Your spouse travels and you dread the days he is gone, not so much because you miss him, but because of the way the kids take advantage of you when he's away.
3. Your spouse is annoyed with your phone calls at work because

you're not handling the problems at home, and he thinks that you're an incompetent parent.

4. Even you are beginning to think that you're incompetent as a parent—or at least ineffective.

5. The kids show their dad respect, but don't seem to appreciate what you do for them.

6. You're contemplating going to work and hiring a sitter so that you don't have to be the one to discipline the children from nine to five.

7. Your parents were harsh with you and your siblings, and you have vowed to give your kids the benefit of the doubt and not punish if possible.

8. Friends tell you to be tougher with the kids, but you ignore their advice because they don't have to live with your children; they "just don't understand."

9. Your husband complains that he feels used—all he's there for is to discipline, and there's little time for fun with the children.

10. The kids tell you they don't like their dad. He's grumpy, rarely talks to them about their day, and acts more like a warden than a father.

Found yourself to be a happiness seeker or a wait-'til-your-father-gets-home parent? If not, there are two other types of parents who are particularly ineffective—those who are uninvolved with their kids (purposefully or inadvertently) and those who are in denial of their children's inappropriate behavior.

The Uninvolved Parent

First, let's take a look at folks who do not spend enough time with their children or give them enough guidance. I'm convinced that parents don't set out to be like this—it subtly evolves, due to many factors. Some folks enter parenthood with very unrealistic expectations about the amount of work, time, and sacrifice it takes to raise children properly. Kids are certainly not like baby turtles who don't even get a glimpse of Mom and are basically on their own from birth. Turtles have well-defined and intense instinctive patterns to guide them and can fend for themselves within the first few minutes of life.

Children, however, have very few survival instincts—they cry and flail about to get their parents' attention, but beyond the attention-getting behavior, they are not wired particularly well for self-survival. Most parents are aware of the physical needs of babies, toddlers, and young children, but are relatively clueless about the emotional nurturing, teaching, and disciplinary needs of their kids. And some parents who are aware of these needs are either too busy, insecure, or emotionally unavailable to train their own children.

Lots of folks have witnessed poor parenting themselves as children, and therefore have the added burden of having to unlearn ineffective parenting techniques and learn some new ones. Still others may know what needs to be done but focus upon other priorities, such as work or social activities, rather than spending time with their kids. Then there's the "hand-'em-to-the-nanny" variety who choose to pay someone to help raise their kids. Now, I'm not suggesting that day care, nannies, or sitters are inappropriate to watch your kids and keep them safe while you're working. Many children enjoy being with other kids in a day care situation and absolutely love their sitters.

But what some people lose sight of is that it's the parents' job to instill values, administer discipline, and serve as role models for their children. It's difficult to do this if the parents are absent a great deal of the time, or are physically at home but mentally elsewhere.

Then there's the large group of folks who are undergoing marital, job, or financial distress and who are so distracted by these problems that there's very little emotional energy left for the kids.

And the list goes on and on. It's tough enough being an effective parent even when life is going smoothly—but it can be downright awful when distractions get in the way. If you find yourself in this category and realize that your degree of involvement with your kids is less than adequate, please do something about it. Of course, you may not be able to quit your job and stay home with the kids (and even if you could, you may not want to!), but be creative and try to think of realistic ways to become more involved with them. It may take the form of reading to them before bedtime, setting a fast-food dinner date with each child individually twice a month, leaving a special note to surprise them in their lunch box at school, or taking walks around the neighborhood together a few times a week, discussing how their lives are going.

Remember—if *you* don't have a significant influence upon them, *someone else* certainly will. Hopefully, it will be someone like a grandparent whom you trust, but it may also turn out to be a group of peers who end up molding your child's value system when he is a teenager. Now that's a scary thought!

My clients, Cassie and Tom, realized almost too late that they had fallen into this pattern of uninvolved parenting. They both had full-time jobs in the city and had to commute over an hour to and from work. Lorna, the live-in nanny, was a godsend to them. She supervised their three-year-old twins on weekdays and was even available to watch the kids during some weekend evenings.

Although this setup seemed to work well (the kids were bathed, fed, and went to the park), Cassie and Tom began to notice that the boys appeared to feel more comfortable and closer to Lorna than to them. Even though they ran to meet their folks at the door as each came home from work, it was Lorna whom they turned to when they weren't feeling well or when they had something especially exciting to report.

Tom and Cassie were beginning to feel left out, and after discussing this situation in therapy, we decided to make some changes in their lifestyle. As a magazine editor, Tom had some flexibility in his schedule—he could work at home a day or two a week—taking breaks during the day and spending time with his sons. Cassie, an assistant comptroller for a merchandising company, arranged to work at her home computer one day a week. She chose a day when Tom wasn't there, so the kids saw at least one of their folks three out of the five workdays and could engage in playtime with them sporadically throughout the day.

Lorna was instrumental in helping the parents keep the "play breaks" under control and also kept the kids occupied when the parent was working in the den. Tom and Cassie also committed to a "Friday fun night" when Lorna was off and just the four of them did something special together. Saturday night was Cassie and Tom's time to spend out together while Lorna took the kids to dinner or watched a video at home with them.

This arrangement satisfied Tom and Cassie's need to become more involved with their kids, but in a way that did not necessitate extreme sacrifice in terms of their careers. It was a compromise, and one that worked out quite well for both the parents and the kids.

Quiz Time

It's easy to fall into the pattern of letting other responsibilities (work, social activities, extended family) compete with your time with your kids. You may be slipping into the pattern of the uninvolved parent if:

1. You just don't seem to have time for everything.
2. Although you make a list, and even put "spending time with the kids" on it, somehow doing the grocery shopping and picking up the dry cleaning takes precedence.
3. You started back to work only part-time, but due to the increased financial needs of raising a family, you've ended up working a forty-hour week—and sometimes more!
4. Although you feel guilty about it, parenting has become a hassle—at least at the office you feel in control. It's just easier to work and let the sitter put up with the kid responsibilities during the day.
5. You've never really been comfortable around babies and toddlers and feel that the day care provider is actually warmer to your two-year-old than you are. You're hoping that by age four, you'll enjoy parenting more and will then spend more time with your child.
6. You don't know what to do with a three-year-old. Even though you don't work outside the home, you find yourself becoming more and more involved in volunteer activities as an excuse to call in a sitter.

7. You long to be with your two kids, but just can't afford not to work the hours you do. Your spouse doesn't want to compromise on lifestyle issues, so you feel trapped into working long hours and not seeing the children as much as you'd like to.

8. You're a single dad and you try as frequently as possible to sneak in extra time with the kids, but you still feel remiss. You feel as if the day care provider is more of a parent to your children than you are.

9. You don't see what all the fuss is about. Your mother-in-law nags at you to spend more time with the children, but you feel that they are getting their needs met—even though you're not the one doing it.

10. Kids really annoy you—they can be demanding and unreasonable and you've found one way to save your sanity is to "hand 'em to the nanny."

The Parent in Denial

One of the toughest types of parents I've come in contact with is the mom and dad in denial regarding their child's inappropriate behavior. Usually, these folks have been warned that if they don't seek counseling for their child, something negative is going to happen, such as their preschooler being expelled from class. I've met many two-, three-, and four-year-olds who have been booted out of a series of preschools for disruptive behavior. The route to expulsion is usually the same. The parents get called in for several conferences, and then different tactics are tried in an attempt to get the child's behavior under control. If the parents do not follow through with the school's suggestions—either because they feel impotent to discipline their child at home for in-school behavior, or they feel that Junior's misbehavior is really the teacher's fault—most schools become fed up and ask the family to leave. That usually gets the parents' attention!

They are shocked into realizing that their kid may have some behavioral flaws and for the first time decide to learn new tactics to use with the child both at home and at school. However, other folks (the particularly thickheaded kind) still don't seem to get it!

Kristi and Richard were a pair of the most defensive parents I had ever met. After their son, Eric, was asked to leave two preschools, they had kept him at home with a sitter the summer before beginning kindergarten. Eric's previous teachers had described his classroom behavior as disruptive and, at times, even wild. When he didn't get his way, he acted out—pushing to be first in line, or hogging the swing, even though other kids were patiently waiting their turn. It was as if the rules didn't apply to Eric and therefore he displayed very poor self-control.

Kristi and Richard, though, preferred to characterize their son as "high-spirited," with a mind of his own. They laughed when he stood up to them and talked back, believing that this was a sign of self-confidence. However, when Eric talked back to me in my office, I felt it to be proof that he was a first-class brat.

Eric's parents took pride in his bossy nature and described his previous teachers as ineffective. After all, Eric did fine at home as long as he was given his way, and his folks resented their son being portrayed by others as having a behavioral problem.

However, when Eric entered kindergarten, his behavior became even more problematic. He was expected to sit at a table without disturbing others, to listen patiently while the teacher was talking, and to refrain from aggressive behavior. It took only four days for his new teacher to realize that she had a live wire on her hands and she immediately called Kristi and Richard in for a conference.

Richard was prepared to give her a piece of his mind about teachers trying to rein in his child's spirit. Apparently, though, this teacher had been around the block a few times herself and had prior experience with defensive parents in denial of their child's behavior. She had prepared documentation listing the times and dates of Eric's infractions, and asked for his parents' cooperation in disciplining their child at home for the misbehavior that occurred at school. Richard became furious that Eric's behavior was being criticized by yet another teacher and he and Kristi stormed out of the meeting.

The next week, they came to see me to help them find a "better school"—one that would encourage Eric's individuality and respect his "spirit." After hearing the history and meeting both the parents and Eric, I could tell that the odds of breaking through their denial were slim. The parents saw nothing wrong with their kid, and so Eric would continue to run the show.

I dutifully listed the various private schools available in our area, but cautioned them that all of these settings had basically the same behavioral expectations for their students, and that unless they helped Eric to learn better self-control, he would soon be in trouble in the new placement. Kristi obviously wasn't getting from me what she wanted, and announced that if no one was willing to respect Eric's individuality that she would "home-school" him.

That was the last I heard from the family, which wasn't surprising. The shame is that Eric is the real victim. He's just responding to the lack of boundaries set up by his folks. Instead of learning self-control from his parents, Eric will have to learn it the hard way—in the school of hard knocks. His folks can avoid irate teachers and school conferences, but they will not be able to escape the judicial system, which I predict this young man is headed for.

When a child grows up believing that rules do not pertain to him, most likely he will not follow them. It will only be a matter of time before even his parents will not be able to save him from the negative consequences caused by his behavior. It's not Eric's fault, but Eric will be the one to pay. Too often I see this pattern and predict that these families will be back to see me when the child is an adolescent and almost totally out of control.

Quiz Time

If you're a parent in denial, you probably won't accept many of these descriptors as relevant to yourself—but let's go for it anyway!

1. Your kid is perfect, plain and simple!
2. Even if your kid is less than perfect, it's not his fault when he messes up—someone else is responsible.
3. You don't trust teachers—they had it in for you when you were growing up and now you feel the same thing is happening with your son.

4. You don't know what to believe when your daughter comes home from kindergarten with a negative note—her story is so believable that you tend to give her the benefit of the doubt and disregard what the teacher has to say.

5. The neighbors are jerks! Neighborhood kids are not allowed to play with yours, but, hey, they're just jealous of Junior—he's not really doing anything wrong (even though he is a bit headstrong).

6. You believe your two-year-old daughter is a handful and even bratty at times, but your spouse becomes angry when you suggest that she may have a problem with her temper. You dislike conflict so much that you've learned not to bring it up with him.

7. You've never been able to take suggestions well yourself—and you perceive most comments about your daughter (both negative and constructive) as a criticism of your parenting ability.

8. If your kid is less than perfect, so are you—and that just won't do.

9. Your parents were very picky about your behavior when you were a kid—you could never do anything right. You've vowed that with your own children, you'd be totally positive and give them the benefit of the doubt when it came to their behavior, and let them off the hook if necessary.

10. Your four-year-old daughter is so cute—how could anyone accuse her of cutting in line or being pushy? She's usually nice to you and the other adults in her life, so what's the teacher griping about anyway?

See yourself as falling into any of these ineffective parenting styles? If so, do something about it! The behavior management techniques presented in chapters 5 and 6 will guide you toward success. Also, check out the following chapter and look for your child's personality type—it may be an eye-opener!

OUTMANIPULATING THE MANIPULATOR

It's two o'clock in the morning and nine-month-old Kary is awake and crying. Her mother wakes up, hovering between sleep and consciousness, hoping that the discomfort is temporary and that baby will soon fall asleep again. After three or four grueling minutes, Mom gives in, takes the baby into her bed, and watches Kary happily cuddle up and fall asleep. Exhausted, as this has become a nightly pattern, Kary's mother tries not to be angry and tries to fall asleep herself. However, her emotions take over and she resentfully wonders how she has allowed this tiny creature to disturb her own sleep habits, leaving her exhausted day after day. Could this lovely, innocent nine-month-old actually be controlling her mother?

Or take four-year-old Sean. He's normally somewhat active but becomes a guided missile as he careens through racks of clothes at the department store. At home, Sean is strong-willed but seems to abide by the rules of the house since he knows that he will be sent to his room if he becomes too rough. However, in the unstructured environment of a mall or store, he seems to lose control and all parental threats appear to fall upon deaf ears. He runs away from his mother, tugs on racks of shirts, and uses the clothing turntable as a playhouse.

How could this child who is so manageable at home lose control so easily when at the department store? Could he actually realize, at the tender age of four years, that his mother's repertoire of consequences is limited outside the home and therefore he perceives the situation as a behavioral free-for-all?

Consider six-year-old Tony. He's recently begun to look depressed, expresses feelings of social rejection, and often forlornly questions what the family would feel like if he had never been born. Instantaneous guilt pangs rush through his parents as they wonder if he is contemplating harming himself. After discussing the situation with each other, the parents note a pattern to Tony's behavior. He seems to look depressed and mention not being part of the family only after being reprimanded for a misdeed or when his parents have not immediately granted a request. Could a youngster of six years actually be manipulating his parents' guilt feelings?

Psychologists have studied phases of children's manipulatory behavior for decades and several interesting patterns have emerged. Babies as young as three months of age understand cause-and-effect relationships, and therefore have the basic tools for budding manipulatory behavior. In addition, as children mature and cognitive ability develops, the nature of child manipulatory tactics becomes more complex, organized, and planned. Unsuspecting parents can become victims of the manipulatory behavior of tyrannical tykes without even realizing it!

The techniques of manipulation become more sophisticated because as the youngster grows, his cognitive and emotional abilities increase. Baby behavior is quite reflexive; babies feel urges that need to be satisfied and their responses tend to be limited to crying, smiling, fussing, and babbling. Very early in their lives, though, even babies learn that adults respond in a predictable fashion. A smile elicits a hug and a smile in return, a giggle elicits a parental laugh, and, most importantly, a scream merits instantaneous parental attention.

This cause-and-effect relationship does not go unnoticed even by the young baby. She is learning more each day what effect her behavior has upon the world around her. Kary, for instance, had been inadvertently trained by her mother to cry loudly when she woke up during the night. She had learned that crying led to being removed from the crib and to being placed in the warmth of her parents' bed.

This cause-and-effect relationship is not coincidental. Kary's experience with her mother taught her that crying elicits immediate attention. As long as her mother continues to react predictably, Kary will continue to awaken and cry during the night.

By the age of four years, the youngster's cognitive abilities are even more highly developed. Four-year-olds can predict consequences, delay immediate gratification of their needs, and selectively control their behavior depending upon the situation.

It is not unusual to hear of a preschooler who behaves appropriately for his teacher but runs his parents ragged at home. The difference lies in the environment. Preschoolers can select their behavior adeptly—controlling themselves in situations where consequences are clear (for instance, at school) and acting out at home if limits are not provided or if the boundaries change daily.

Remember Sean, careening through the department store? He exemplifies the typical four-year-old who is already a professional at manipulating his mother. Sean knows what behaviors he can get away with depending upon the situation he finds himself in. At home, he knows that his mother will utilize one or more of several punishments for inappropriate behavior. He has experienced spankings, time-out in his bedroom, as well as the loss of television privileges. But Sean realizes that his mother's attention is easily diverted at the store. He knows that he can wander and get into things and that her bag of parental tricks is limited when away from home, so he grabs the opportunity to act out when the consequences for his inappropriate behavior are unclear. Parents should never underestimate the creative manipulatory behavior of their kids. The trick is to "outmanipulate the manipulator" and to not fall prey to the incredibly persistent control tactics youngsters possess.

And consider Tony, the six-year-old who realized that expressing feelings of social rejection generally resulted in parental guilt feelings as well as extra attention. Tony is a manipulatory champ. He can knock the wind out of a parent with a single comment. His behavior exemplifies the manipulatory tactic of using feelings of sadness to gain control or attention. Children quickly perceive their parents' hot buttons, and guilt provocation is a good example. The parent who perceives his child as sad or depressed can be easily overwhelmed by the child's displayed emotion and fall into the trap of feeling responsible for the youngster's negative self-statements. The child who employs this maneuver is especially cagey, as he keeps his parents on edge, knowing they don't want to upset him.

Outmanipulating the Manipulator: Understanding Children's Manipulative Styles

The first step in dealing with kid manipulatory behavior is to realize that even very young children can select their emotions and behaviors based upon the reaction they wish to receive from the adult. Once you accept the notion of child manipulation, you can become a more effective disciplinarian and not fall prey as frequently to children's tactics. However, no matter how consistent you try to be as a parent, some kids are always looking for loopholes in the rules. Others will behave only if the consequence affects them intensely, and still others will spite themselves just to prove who the boss is. These kids are manipulative pros and fall within several categories.

The If-Then Child

Many little kids are what I call if-then children. They behave appropriately only when there is something in it for them. Jamie was a classic—four years old and already a manipulative pro. If asked to clean up her toys, she would do it only if her mother, Carole, followed her request with the threat of a negative consequence. She would get in the bath only if Carole told her that there would be no bedtime snack if she didn't comply.

Carole was a member of a single-parent support group that I met with on a weekly basis. The other parents would nod in agreement as she described the countless times during the day that Jamie would push her to the limit and respond only if threatened with a negative consequence. It was tough to run such a household, especially after working all day, picking Jamie up from day care, and then having to stay one step ahead of her throughout the evening. Carole was exhausted. At least they made it through the week, but Carole worried that she had caused her daughter's stubbornness and questioned her own parenting ability.

Carole wondered aloud if she would have to couch all requests of Jamie with an if-then statement for the next fourteen years. I told her that there was a good chance that she would—since a dyed-in-the-wool if-then kid often needs to understand the consequence before deciding how to act. However, I've seen many of these kids evolve into more reasonable children as they mature, as long as they know that the if-then connection continues to exist. Carole will make it through Jamie's childhood and adolescence—it may not be easy and will most likely be exhausting. But if she stays the consistent disciplinarian she is, Jamie will most likely understand the rules and behave appropriately, if only to avoid the consequences of misbehavior. Even though parents might not state it each time, kids can predict from experience what will happen to them if they don't respond properly. Hopefully, as Jamie matures, she will come to understand and accept the need to cooperate with others. Even if she continues to behave appropriately only to avoid negatives, that's a heck of a lot better than putting up with a kid who completely ignores requests.

In my experience, the if-then kid is perhaps the most common type of manipulator. Misbehavior and noncompliance are characteristics of if-then kids, and many children fall within this category at some point in their lives.

Parents continually claim that this was not the way it was when they were growing up. There are various versions of the tale, but most proceed as follows: "When I was a kid I wouldn't have dared to talk back to my parents, or my father would have walloped me." Another rendition: "I did what my mother asked me to do just because she was my mom, and I was expected to comply." No doubt there are many adults today who truly acted appropriately as children. However, there were many if-then children in their generation also.

Most of us were acquainted with if-then kids as we were growing up. These were the youngsters who continually broke rules and tried to push the limits as much as possible. If their parents or teachers were not successful at consistently applying consequences for unacceptable behaviors, these if-then children of long ago have most likely evolved into if-then adults today.

If-then adults still continue to need rules to keep their behavior appropriate. "*If* you have an affair, *then* I will leave you" is a typical statement of the wife of an if-then husband. This threat may or may not be successful, depending upon whether the if-then husband values the marital relationship. Another version is "*If* you do not come to work on time, *then* I will fire you." Too many if-then employees lose their jobs because the threat of being without work is not important enough to them, or they are lacking in the self-control necessary to follow the rules given by the employer.

The parents of an if-then child need to depend less upon their perception of the way they acted toward their parents when they were children and to focus more upon the ways in which their own kid is behaving. To expect your child to be reasonable because "that's the way it should be" or "that's the way I was for my parents" may be unrealistic. Practical parenting involves perceiving your kids in a realistic manner and developing appropriate expectations for them.

If a parent is lucky enough to have a reasonable child, talking with the youngster will most likely be effective. Although even the most reasonable of children can become if-then kids occasionally, if the frequency of acting out is low, occasional outbursts are generally tolerable.

It is the child who continually needs the if-then parental approach who wears down the parent. The adult must persevere, always responding with very clear rules. This is necessary if the parent is to continue to control the situation. When the parent becomes exhausted and gives in, the child will manipulate even more. In other words, the adult must learn to outmanipulate the manipulator.

There are three other types of children who are capable of driving their parents crazy and who will benefit from more structure in their lives. Two of them, the power-hungry tyrant and the dependent heart wrencher, tend to be experts at manipulation. The third category, the chameleon kid, displays behavioral problems more as a reaction to fuzzy or nonexistent parental rules than as a maneuver to control the situation. Let's take a look at each of these kids, starting with the latter, which is the most common.

The Chameleon Kid

Chameleon kids are children who respond to the rules of whatever environment they find themselves in. When given adequate rules and structure, they generally will comply well, and some people may swear that they are angelic. But in a situation without sufficient rules or consistent guidelines, these kids may become noncompliant or disruptive.

Take my clients Charles and Suzanne. They told me of their recent meeting with four-year-old Meghan's preschool teacher, Mrs. Dowells.

The teacher described Meghan as a curious, intelligent young lady who loved playing in the various learning centers and on the playground with the other kids. In the conference, Mrs. Dowells read the parents a laundry list of Meghan's crimes—talking back, pushing in line to become number one, and even instigating food fights at lunch. She felt that Meghan understood the class rules, but deliberately chose to ignore or break them when she felt like it. The school policy for misbehavior was to place the child in the time-out chair for three minutes, or to sit next to the teacher on the bench while the other kids played on the playground. If these consequences failed, the parents were called in for a conference.

Mrs. Dowells noted that she was concerned about Meghan's disruptive and rude behavior, as well as her own inability to keep the classroom under control when Meghan let loose with some of her antics. It was a large class, and even with the help of an aide, Mrs. Dowells was at her wits' end.

Charles and Suzanne listened to the teacher but felt that she was talking about another little girl, not their Meghan. If her behavior became out of hand at home, she was warned that if she continued to misbehave, she would lose TV privileges for the remainder of the day.

Since Meghan loved watching cartoons, she became very upset when this privilege was taken away from her. Suzanne and Charles felt in control of their daughter at home, but didn't know how to help Mrs. Dowells to gain control of Meghan during the school day.

The school referred Charles and Suzanne to me to help with the situation. After getting to know Meghan, it was clear that she was a classic chameleon kid—the type of child whose behavior is based on the environment she finds herself in, just like the chameleon changes colors depending upon the twig he finds himself upon.

At home, her parents were quick to give consequences for inappropriate actions, and Meghan had connected her behavior with the punishments that followed. Because she was able to control her behavior when she wanted to, she did—at least at home.

I described to the family how clever Meghan was to be able to distinguish the differences between home and school and that she misbehaved for Mrs. Dowells because she was able to get away with it. The teacher's hands were tied—she couldn't take away Meghan's television privileges since they didn't watch TV at school, and sitting for three minutes in the time-out chair was apparently not that uncomfortable for Meghan. She could still watch the other kids play and the three minutes went by quickly.

Meghan was a very nice kid, but a bit manipulative in nature. She could be cooperative if motivated, but became ornery if there was no consequence for her stubbornness. To control Meghan's behavior, Mrs. Dowells needed to be creative and to figure out some motivators to use with her. Admittedly, it would be more difficult than at home— but I assured the family that it could be accomplished.

I suggested setting up consequences at school that might matter to Meghan, as well as adding to that a home consequence that she would receive each day from her parents. Combined, I predicted that Meghan's behavior at school would improve, keeping her actions within a tolerable zone.

The negative consequences I suggested for school were longer time-outs (ten to fifteen minutes in a spot that was less interesting, perhaps in the secretary's office), losing the special treat in her lunch box that day, or having to spend recess time in the two-year-olds' room while her friends played on the playground. And when Mom or Dad picked her up, they would be given a daily report of her behavior. If it was good, they might choose to stop for a treat on the way home, or if the report was negative, she would lose her television privileges that evening. In this way, Mrs. Dowells had a collection of motivators to use that just might get Meghan's attention and teach her to think about her school behavior before acting on impulse, just as she had proven she could do at home.

If your child is a chameleon kid, be prepared to set up significant structure in her life. This may take the form of weeding out friends who are not good influences, choosing teachers who are structured, and setting up a clear and comprehensive daily schedule of what you expect each day from your child. Chameleon kids tend to need black-and-white situations; ambiguity or shades of gray allow the child to slip through loopholes. Try to predict "cracks" in the child's schedule and expectations and fill them so that she can't slip through.

The Power-Hungry Tyrant

Marshall and Janet came to the conclusion around Nathan's second birthday that they had seriously goofed when they named their son Nathan—the consensus was that "Napoleon" would have been more appropriate. This kid was not only stubborn, but tyrannical to boot. Not only did Nathan have to have sole possession of his own toys but he also laid claim to everyone else's possessions. By three and one-half years of age, Nathan had established a neighborhood reputation as a power-hungry tyrant. It was his way or no way! The other kids had to play the games he wanted to play, and, of course, he called the shots—rules changed to meet his needs, and Nathan never conceded defeat. By age four, very few kids wanted to play with Nathan—it was just too much trouble and not really fun to put up with all of his changing rules.

When his folks tried to explain to him how his tyrannical ways turned others off, Nathan would become very defensive and blame everyone else for provoking his actions. Not only did he have very little insight into the cause-and-effect relationship between his behaviors and others' reactions, he really wasn't interested in changing. Nathan wanted the world around him to change; he wasn't going to budge an inch.

This kid was a pro at trying to make others take responsibility for his anger and frustration. When someone would tread on his turf or he didn't get what he wanted, Nathan would throw such a fit that his parents, sitters, or peers often caved in and gave him his way. It just wasn't worth standing up to him. The kids learned to avoid him and to play with others, but Marshall and Janet realized that they were in this for the long haul and needed to find a better way of coping with, if not changing, his behaviors and attitudes.

Reasoning with Nathan obviously didn't work—it was like talking to a wall. He rationalized losing friends by blaming them for the bickering that inevitably occurred when someone came over and tried to play with him. So, appealing to Nathan's sense of fair play, sensitivity, and willingness to change was a dead end. A different approach would have to be taken.

I suggested to Marshall and Janet that some kids are as stubborn as donkeys and will risk losing everything in order to save face and not admit that they are wrong. What might work better for their family would be to turn the tables on Nathan—to get him to see control not in terms of being so nasty that he would run off his friends or anger his parents, but to teach him that true control was being able to work with others so that his needs were met while not harming them.

Nathan obviously wanted to be a leader, but he always went about it the wrong way. His folks needed to teach him that if he wanted to control a play situation in a positive way, a little preplanning could do the trick. Instead of inviting kids over and then defending his turf (mostly games and toys), Nathan could make available only those things that he was willing to share that day. He could take solace in realizing that his other treasures were safely put away. The point was that he was still calling the shots, yet in a manner that didn't offend the other kids. Nathan would soon realize that this attitude would net him not only the control of his property he so desired, but that he would also remain in control of his social relationships.

Power-hungry tyrants often don't see alternatives to their aggressive behavior. They view sharing even an inch of their turf as a defeat. Teaching them that working with others leads to even greater control is an inviting enticement and many little kids soon pick up on this new behavior and run with it!

The Dependent Heart Wrencher

Karen's mom, Nancy, felt as if she was joined at the hip with her three-year-old daughter. As a baby, Karen would let no one but her mom or baby-sitter hold her without pitching a fit. Not even Alex, her father, could pick her up without the child whining and fussing, holding her arms out to her mother to be rescued. Early on, Karen's folks felt it was too much trouble to fight her on this issue and Nancy would give in, drop what she was doing, and grab up the child. After a few assorted whimpers, Karen would quiet down and mold into her mother's arms, finally content. Karen had become what I call a dependent heart wrencher.

Nancy and Alex told me at our first interview that Karen had begun this behavior around the time she had turned five months of age. Before that, she had allowed friends and relatives to hold her without much of a fuss. Nancy had returned to work part-time when the baby was six weeks old and Karen had adjusted to the baby-sitter who watched her for five or six hours a day. But right around five months, Karen began fussing and crying if someone other than her mother tried to hold her. As she became older, she would run to Nancy to hide behind her legs, but once her mother picked her up and held her, she would relax and look at the stranger—as long as Nancy continued to hold her in her arms. Alex felt somewhat miffed by Karen's rejections, but since she seemed so frightened when held by anyone other than her mom or baby-sitter, he learned not to take it personally and chalked her behavior up to insecurity. Since at that time she had only one child, Nancy was able to pick Karen up and hold her as she went about her household chores or returned the day's phone calls.

However, when Karen was almost three years old, Nancy became pregnant again. She had spoken about the situation to Karen's pediatrician, who was well aware of the child's "mommy-itis." Even the doctor had difficulty examining Karen and often had to pry her out of Nancy's arms and pin her to the examination table in order to give her a checkup. The pediatrician agreed that Karen needed to learn some "independence behavior" before the new baby was born, since Nancy would not be able to hold two kids at once. The doctor had referred the family to me for consultation in order to teach them techniques to help change Karen's overly dependent behavior.

I interviewed Nancy and Alex during the first session, and asked them to bring Karen in next. She wouldn't separate from her parents in the waiting room, so I interviewed her in my office while she sat on her mother's lap. Karen didn't have much to say and she refused to leave Nancy's lap to play with the blocks and other toys on the floor. However, I saw her eyeing them as I spoke to her and knew that she was interested in the toys. It was obvious that Karen was conflicted— the curious child wanted to check out the enticing toys, but the frightened, anxious little girl prevented her from doing so. When I handed her some ponies to play with, she seemed satisfied and began to relax. Karen even answered some of my questions about her favorite toys, videos, and friends, as the ponies distracted her from her fears.

I could tell that this child had been born with a threat-sensitive nature, easily intimidated, yet eager to please. She appeared to be bright and curious, but her anxieties paralyzed her, keeping her from exploring her world. Karen was exhibiting a chronic case of separation anxiety—a normal phase that many babies temporarily experience beginning around the fifth or sixth month of age. But Karen had taken this to an extreme, developing the dependent-heart-wrencher behavior pattern.

Because of her extremely sensitive temperament, as well as Nancy's constant giving in to her clinging behavior, Karen had not yet outgrown this dependent phase of development and was not learning to be independent. I agreed with the pediatrician that it was important to help her to become more secure with herself before the new baby arrived.

At our next session, we set up a system of "successive approximations"—a list of small steps that Karen could take that would eventually lead to more independent behaviors. First, I asked Alex to pick Karen up from the sitter's house, even though Nancy had always been the one to do that. Initially, Karen was reluctant to go with Alex, but since she wanted to go home, she went along with it. The next step involved Alex taking Karen to her favorite fast-food place for dinner on their way home. This went well as she loved "kids' meals" as well as playing in the outdoor playground while Alex watched her.

Alex began to relax as he became able to count on Karen going willingly to the car with him and enjoying herself while they ate. When they arrived home, Karen would run to her mother, hug her, and tell her what she and Daddy had eaten and how they had played with the other kids.

The next step involved Alex taking Karen on small errands with him. At first, Karen was anxious as he led her to the car, but after a few trips, she went willingly. Karen would have preferred to have gone with her mother, but she was beginning to accept spending time alone with her dad. Alex did a good job of not getting upset by her rejections and would divert her attention by talking to her and playing her audio tapes in the car.

The next step was to arrange for Karen to begin preschool. She had played daily with three other kids at the sitter's house and had gotten along well with them. It was now time for her to learn to deal with a teacher and a larger group of children as her independence grew.

Nancy took Karen to visit the chosen preschool for an hour one day. According to Nancy, Karen looked conflicted—she wanted to play with the toys but instead she clung to her mother's knees. Nancy told me at our session the next day that Karen seemed to be taking everything in, that she wanted to participate but couldn't from her perch hidden behind her mother.

We decided that Karen was ready for half-day preschool and that she would begin the next day. Alex would take her to school instead of Nancy, as it might be easier for Karen to leave Dad rather than Mom. The parents fretted all evening but stuck to the plan as Alex brought her to school the next morning. Nancy later noted that it was one of the most difficult things she had to do as a parent, but realized that Karen needed to become more independent even if it had to be forced upon her!

That afternoon, Alex called me to report that Karen had a difficult time at school. She had cried as he left and the teacher noted that she continued to be upset until the sitter picked her up at noon. We decided to stick with the plan, though, and talked positively with Karen that evening about going to school the next morning. Nancy worried that we were putting too much pressure on Karen but agreed to try it for a few more days.

Luckily, day two went much better. Karen cried when Alex left, but the teacher was able to match her up with Jenny, a rather outgoing child who immediately took over and showed Karen the ropes of preschool. At noon, the sitter had to search the playground for Karen when she came to pick her up, and finally found her and Jenny digging in the sandbox together. Karen was more than willing to leave, but said good-bye to Jenny and her teacher before hopping in the car.

It was good that Karen had such a positive experience because I doubt that Nancy would have made her go to school the next day if she'd had another difficult time. Karen soon adjusted to the half-day school routine and eventually was able to be dropped off by her mother, since the preschool was actually on her way to work. She didn't cry when Nancy dropped her off, but gave her a kiss and ran to find Jenny.

I've seen the family twice since that fateful second day of school, and Karen continues to become more independent. She will most likely continue to be more sensitive than most kids, but that trait can come in handy in social relationships. Nancy noted that she is now aware of her own tendency to overprotect Karen and continues to force herself to allow the child to experience some social anxiety when she feels that it will be a learning experience for her daughter.

I received a phone call about a month after our last appointment. Karen herself talked to me on the telephone to announce that baby Joshua had been born and that he and her mother would be coming home from the hospital the next day. She also told me that she couldn't wait to take him to school for show-and-tell!

The dependent heart wrencher is a difficult kid, not purposefully manipulative like the if-then child or the power-hungry tyrant, but tough in other ways. It's easy for parents to fall into the trap of giving in to the child's dependency and clinging—she appears to need the extra comforting and attention. It's hard, though, to draw the line between giving just the right amount of comforting versus crossing over the line and blocking the child's opportunities to learn independence. If you feel that the line has been crossed with your child, try setting up a program of "successive approximations," as did Nancy and Alex. It will work if the steps are small and you stick to the program.

All of these manipulative kids are trying to parents at the least, and downright awful in some cases. But whether your child is an if-then kid, dependent heart wrencher, chameleon kid, or a power-hungry tyrant, the solution tends to be the same. You need to set up clear guidelines and consequences and to stick to the program. You are, after all, quite capable of taking control, but you may not have realized how to use the creative parenting powers you possess.

Keeping or taking back control of your kid is a lot easier than living with a manipulative child. It may be tough at first to turn the tables on him, but once you have his attention and he realizes that you will do something (not just lecture or nag or try to reason), you'll see much greater cooperation and compliance, and significantly less manipulation.

BEHAVIOR MANAGEMENT

The Benevolent Dictator: The Parenting Style That Works

The manipulative kids discussed in the last chapter all have one characteristic in common—in different ways, they are all trying to run the show, often without taking into account the effect their behaviors have upon others. In my practice, I have found that parenting as a benevolent dictator (kindly letting your children know that they have a vote, but that you are the final decision maker), rather than parenting as a "democracy" (often a free-for-all), to be the most effective manner of teaching children frustration tolerance and self-control. The parent has greater control and establishes more stability in the home. In his book *Parent Power! A Common-Sense Approach to Parenting in the '90s and Beyond*, John Rosemond suggests that benevolent dictators do not "demand unquestioning obedience. They encourage questions, but make the final decisions. They restrict their children's freedom, but they are not tyrants. They restrict in order to protect and guide. . . . Life with a Benevolent Dictator is predictable and secure for children." In choosing a benevolent dictatorship, the parent understands that although he may feel guilty and perhaps sorry for the child when he has to be punished, the kid will profit from receiving the consequence rather than being taught the wrong lesson—that misbehavior will be tolerated.

Kids learn self-control when parents create boundaries and set limits. The familiar expression "It was almost as if he was asking to be punished" is quite apt. One often sees children who appear to be more content after limits have been set for them. Children usually do not ask for limit setting, but their moods tend to improve when they know what they can get away with and what they can't.

For example, five-year-old Stacey constantly begged her parents to allow her to eat dinner in front of the TV set, while the rest of the family sat at the dinner table. She started such a fuss that they finally gave in. But her folks resented that she wasn't willing to put being part of the family above catching a few more cartoons. After attending counseling and learning about limit setting, her parents were able to set more strict guidelines. Stacey was told to be at the table by a certain time each night and if she refused she was placed in time-out until she was willing to sit with the family. After a week of this regimen, she came to the table on her own accord, and actually happily engaged in the conversation. This worked because Stacey's parents were willing to risk conflict with her in order to do what they felt was best for her and the other kids.

Do all folks need to parent as a benevolent dictator? It depends. Some lucky parents have easy children (babies who sleep through the night, toddlers who add "okay" and "yes" to their vocabularies, grade schoolers who do their homework without too many parental threats, middle schoolers who believe that trying drugs is a stupid idea, high schoolers who still talk to their parents and perhaps even listen to them once in a while, and adult children who leave home without having to be kicked out). These types of kids I like to call keepers. They probably can be raised in a more democratic household because they naturally tend not to abuse others or to take advantage of situations. You may know a family blessed with a youngster who appears by nature to be reasonable. But although these easygoing, self-motivated youngsters do exist, they appear to be the exception rather than the rule.

In his book *Nature of the Child,* psychologist Jerome Kagan cites many studies showing that temperament is largely inborn. For example, babies who are born with a tendency toward extreme timidity tend to remain shy and inhibited as they mature. This does not mean that once the child's "blueprint" has been ascertained that the parent should meekly accept it—"My child was ornery from the beginning, and therefore this is a lost cause." In fact, quite the opposite is true.

Environmental influence plays a very important part in molding personality and behavior. Easy children may need less molding—just a firm look from the parent may do the trick. Difficult children may need more guidance, such as time-outs, or having privileges removed. The trick is to determine as early as possible which type of child you are raising and to use this information to develop your own disciplinary plan.

Even the most compliant child often reaches a testy stage when he digs his heels in and demands unreasonable privileges. You'll realize that this has occurred when you feel yourself in conflict with your child even after you've tried to be reasonable, explained your decision thoroughly, and she still sees it only from her perspective. Some kids reach this stage later than others, but most will eventually evidence some rebellious behavior. Parents need to be able to recognize the testy stage as a normal phase of development and to deal with it effectively.

So, whether your child is an easygoing, compliant kid or one who makes his living giving you gray hair, it's necessary to develop a behavioral plan. Consistent, effective discipline given in a nonchalant manner is the trick. Just the thought of this may sound overwhelming. Parents with overcontrolling, unself-disciplined children find it difficult to imagine that they can even come close to achieving this goal.

Somewhere between the ages of two and three years, kids become capable of understanding perfectly well what their limits are if their parents set boundaries for them. Limits should follow the four *c*'s. They must be *concise, clear, consistent,* and—at times—*catastrophic.*

Concise and clear limits are mandatory in terms of rule setting because children have a way of finding loopholes. The youngster who has been told not to tease his younger brother may resort to driving his little sister crazy. His indignant retort to the parent who wishes to punish him may be "You told me not to tease my brother, but you didn't say anything about teasing my sister!" Parents can easily become exasperated by this type of manipulation and should establish rules in broad and encompassing terms such as, *"Never tease your siblings!"*

Children are human computers when keeping mental track of parental inconsistencies, so consequences for inappropriate behaviors should be applied *consistently*. For example, the child may say, "You didn't punish me yesterday for bugging my brother, so it's unfair to send me to my room today." The child does have a point. The parent is sending mixed messages, and the child will use this to his advantage.

Dr. Fitzhugh Dodson suggests in his book *How to Discipline with Love: From Crib to College* that successful parents believe that how they parent directly affects how their children behave, and accordingly they take care to discipline their kids consistently. Second, they are not afraid to confront their children, even if this means a temporary rift between the parent and child. The parents' ability to put negative emotions from the child ("I hate you for sending me to my room!") into proper perspective is essential. Consistent discipline (the teaching of rules and consequences for maintaining or breaking rules) appears to be the key element.

The last *c* involves catastrophic consequences. I'm not advocating corporal punishment. Personally, I believe that kids respond better to other negative consequences, such as time-out, but I have met families in my practice who swear that a pop on the butt (or even just the threat of it) works wonders. There are many other consequences you can use that will get your kid's attention and lead to considerably better behavior, but the consequences have to be *important* to the child in order to have an effect.

Behavior Management Ground Rules

Most families with noncompliant children have tried everything before seeking professional advice. Disciplinary tactics that they have employed often include spanking, time-out, removing privileges, and—most notable—lecturing.

Parents often tell me that each of these consequences seems to work for a short time, but the effectiveness soon dissipates. Generally, they give in and stop the punishment due to their own guilt or exhaustion. Parents come to the counselor's office at their wits' end, looking for a magic cure. But they find that magic does not exist. The solution involves common sense and lots of effort but is quite workable if they are willing to take some chances, stand up to their kids, and learn the basics of managing their children's behavior. What follows is a discussion of the basic ground rules parents need to use in order for a behavior management program to work.

Consistency

First, let's explore consistency. Most parents try to follow through with the rules they do establish, but many succumb to the sabotaging techniques of their kids.

Youngsters are professionals at wearing parents down, and why shouldn't they be? They have more energy and fewer responsibilities than adults and can be very persistent in order to get their way. My client, three-year-old Jonathan, cried every time his parents turned off the TV to start the bedtime ritual. On nights when they were determined that Jonathan would meet the bedtime, they stuck to their guns and made sure that the bath was taken and Jonathan hit the sack on time. More often, though, Jonathan's folks caved in to his cries of protest and let him fall asleep on the floor, watching television. Later, they would carry him into the bedroom—teeth unbrushed and body unbathed.

Or take six-year-old Nicholas. His parents had a set rule regarding snacking before dinner. Nicholas was not to have any food after 5:00 P.M. because when he snacked, he tended to pick at his dinner and not finish it. Nicholas, the cagey, manipulative pro that he was, realized that if he bugged his mother enough about snacks while she was occupied taking care of the baby, she often gave in and he had free run of the pantry. Sometimes, she stood firm and continued to say no, but more often than not, she acquiesced. Nicholas's mother, therefore, had actually taught him to bug, nag, and not take no for an answer because hassling usually paid off for him. She was actually teaching her son to be manipulative due to her inconsistency!

Also, be careful about threatening consequences that you cannot follow through with. Don't threaten to remove your daughter's TV privileges for a year, because you probably won't. A week is easy to do and still stings. To remain consistent, you may have to soften the consequence a bit in order to guarantee that you'll really follow through with it.

Effective Consequences

Disciplinary tactics that are effective for one family may not work well for another. The effectiveness of any consequence varies depending upon factors such as the number of kids in the family, the children's ages, and the home environment.

In determining if a consequence will work for you, ask yourself, "Will *this* consequence make an impression on *this* child?" If it is a reward, is it appealing to the particular youngster? Meghan may love new books, whereas Laurie couldn't care less about them. Television, playtime, and food treats may be rewarding to some kids, while others treasure time with you or use of the computer.

Negative consequences also must make an impression. The issue regarding punishments should be "Will *this* punishment be meaningful to *this* child and bother him enough so that the inappropriate behavior decreases?" Five minutes of time-out normally will not affect a five-year-old, but fifteen minutes should, and if it doesn't, thirty minutes spent in time-out may make the kid think twice!

Tailoring the consequences to the individual child is mandatory. A child who practically lives for television will change almost any inappropriate behavior if television privileges are threatened, while another youngster may respond more to taking away her favorite books or hobbies. The five-year-old boy who is obsessed with cartoons, the four-year-old girl addicted to Gummi Bears, and the six-year-old miser saving up quarters for a new toy will all respond if these particular motivators are used.

Negative Consequences

Taking Away

Families have many types of negative consequences available to them. Loss of possessions, attention, and privileges are common. For instance, permanently taking away a toy or two most likely will get your child's attention, and she'll begin to believe that you mean business in the future. Most parents, however, do not take away enough or make the loss significant—losing TV time for an hour can easily be tolerated by a six-year-old, but loss of all "electricity" (TV, Nintendo, and computer) for an entire day really has an impact! Too often, however, we continue to use inconsequential punishments over and over again, without being creative or imposing other possibly more effective measures.

Time-Out

Time-out is both a physical and a psychological condition. Physically, a time-out setting is a safe place where the child must go for a specified period of time. Psychologically, time-out is the placement of the child away from all attention and interesting activities. This allows the kid to consider what rule she has broken in order to have been placed in time-out, as well as to think about how to avoid being put there again in the near future.

Setting

The optimal time-out situation is an empty bedroom, but most rooms will suffice if they are emptied of interesting or potentially dangerous objects. One must be concerned with scissors, medications, etc., and remove these from the room, since the child, when placed in time-out, may be quite angry and inadvertently harm himself. Place the child in the time-out room for a set period of time. The amount of time varies according to the age and personality of the child. Parents often hear from their pediatricians that they should allow one minute of time-out for each year of the child's age. In my experience, four minutes for a four-year-old probably won't make a dent. You may find that doubling that amount of time will get your kid's attention. The five-year-old may need fifteen minutes, whereas the six-year-old usually needs at least half an hour of time-out for his misdeed to sink in. Especially ornery kids may require an hour of time-out in order to gain their attention.

Keeping the Child in Time-Out

Some kids need to have the door closed during time-out since they tend to leave the room. If the child opens the door and leaves the room, then the door may need to be locked from the outside. This will eliminate parents' having to become physically involved in putting the child back in time-out. (Due to their immaturity, it is not advisable to put a child under age three in a room with the door closed, let alone locked. A tall baby gate placed in the doorway keeps them in, and you can supervise their behavior.)

I suggest that you give little or no attention to your kid during time-out. Youngsters need to learn that their parents are in control and will resort to placing them in a boring, safe situation when they lose self-control or become overly demanding. If an empty bedroom is not available, a safe bathroom or the child's own bedroom may suffice.

It is important to remember that the purpose of time-out is to gain the child's attention, not to place him in a harmful environment. Whenever the time-out situation is employed, it must be safe, boring, well lit, and well ventilated. Time-out is effective because it bores the child, not because it harms him.

Some especially tough kids tend to be angrier after time-out than they were when they went in. Often after time-out they will fuss, kick, and hit just to let you know who's the boss. This is a great excuse to practice your new nonchalant attitude. You can quietly let your child know that if she continues to misbehave, then she will be placed back in time-out if the inappropriate behavior doesn't stop. Score one for Mom or Dad!

Use of the Timer

The use of a kitchen timer is very helpful when employing time-out as a negative consequence. The timer is placed outside the room and is set for the allotted period. The child knows that time-out is over when the buzzer rings and that the parent will remove him from the situation only at that time. This eliminates the need for you to constantly respond to the child's persistent questions: "Is it time yet?" or "When can I come out?" When the buzzer rings, time-out is over.

The less you communicate with your kid during time-out, the better. If your kid perceives that he has you upset, he may feel that he has won the conflict. In reality, no one wins in control disputes. These situations should be looked upon as learning experiences, not as notches on a gun barrel by either the parent or the youngster. You'll soon experience that time-out is a very powerful technique that will help you regain your composure and emphasize to the child that you truly are in control.

Positive Consequences

In terms of rewarding kids, parents have several effective options. Activity, social, and material rewards are the most common reinforcers.

Activity Rewards

Activity or privilege rewards can be quite effective with kids. Little kids enjoy playing board games, watching videos, or taking a trip to the park. Grade schoolers like playing video games, spending time with their friends, or going for a bike ride. Again, be sure that the activity you choose is one that your child enjoys and values.

Social Rewards

Social rewards are parental behaviors such as praise and attention. Kids crave their parents' approval and will work to receive it. Some prefer being praised for a job well done, whereas others often secretly enjoy a hug or a good-natured "noogie" to the head.

Material Rewards

The third major type of reward involves giving material objects. Most kids will work for material rewards such as toys or money. Often I suggest using poker chips in lieu of cash—they are easier to use and to keep track of. Instead of a weekly allowance given without strings attached, a daily "cash" poker chip can be earned if the child has displayed appropriate behavior. If using toys as a reward, the parent determines how much should be earned before taking a trip to the toy store. The child can earn one toy poker chip per day as part of a behavior management system. This amount is to be saved and spent for toys only.

One of the outcomes of this technique is that children learn to spend money wisely. Initially, many four-, five-, and six-year-olds tend to be extravagant and buy expensive toys. However, when the child realizes that the parent is not going to be buying any other toys, the child begins to look for less expensive items and will become more prudent in spending her own money, learning this lesson even at a young age.

I caution parents not to interfere with the child's selections. She has to learn how to handle spending money herself, even if mistakes are made at the beginning of the poker chip system. If you let her make her own decisions, she'll learn to take responsibility for mistakes and not blame errors of judgment on you.

Parental Nonchalance

Parents need to practice the fine art of parental nonchalance. Saying calmly, "If you don't stop tantrumming, I'll give away your favorite toy" and walking away is a good example. If the child continues to throw a fit, take the toy away and the child does not get it back.

If you aren't nonchalant, you'll be sure prey for your youngster, because kids love to push their parents' hot buttons. What could be more controlling (and amusing) than merely talking back to an adult and seeing the parent's face flush, arms move frantically, and teeth clench? Some children delight in the control they gain when they can cause so many physiological changes in an adult! It's almost worth the punishment. The nonchalant parent, though, informs the youngster of the transgression and the consequence and then enforces the punishment, quickly and without flinching. Score one for Mom!

Sound easy? Not necessarily. It may take weeks of practice, but the payoffs are enormous. Children will no longer feel they earn points for getting their parents angry; they will receive only negative consequences.

I've found that couples often seem to have an easier time achieving nonchalance than do single parents. When they feel that they are becoming unglued, one parent can hand the situation over to the other, take a break, and reenter after having gained her composure. Single parents have to figure out a way to take a time-out for themselves if they feel that they are losing their composure, and come back to the situation after they have cooled down. Whether you are a single parent or have a partner, concurrent use of consistent, effective discipline given in a nonchalant manner allows you to gain (or to regain) control, and the family will become a more organized, pleasant unit.

Rule Setting

Before we proceed to setting up the Smiley Face system in chapter 6, a presentation of general rule-setting techniques is in order. When disciplining kids, be sure to:

*Consistently reward good behavior and do so immediately.

*Punish inappropriate behavior with use of an effective negative consequence.

*Be careful not to reward inappropriate behavior.

*Follow Grandma's rule: "First work, then play."

Let's look at each of these. Rewarding good behavior and punishing inappropriate behavior are very important. For example, the parent who has been struggling with his kid to take a bath without a hassle is an all too typical scenario. One evening, though, the youngster turns off the television and goes with the parent to the bathtub without complaining. Instead of ignoring this success, the parent chooses to note it by praising the child immediately. The child feels good and so does his father! However, had the child continued to complain and procrastinate, his father should have given him a negative consequence (such as no bedtime story that night) because his son had previously been warned that complaints about taking a bath would no longer be tolerated.

The third point is that the parent who gives in to her child's constant hassling and complaining actually rewards the undesirable behavior. Kids have a tremendous ability to persevere. They can hassle a parent endlessly, especially if in the past, the parent has given in to the child's demands. Be sure that your kids' whining *never* results in their getting what they want. Then they will learn to rephrase their complaints into appropriate requests.

The fourth point, and a very important principle in rule setting, is that behavior leading to rewards will continue, whereas behavior that is not rewarded will cease. This principle is commonly referred to as Grandma's rule, most likely because our foremothers were pretty smart cookies and employed it liberally. Grandma's rule states, "After you do your work, then you will get to play," or in practice, "After you clean up your room, then you can watch television or go outside."

All too often, though, parents tend to reverse Grandma's rule in terms of negotiating with their kids. For instance, the child may promise that he will clean up his room if only he can play a video game first. As many parents find out, the odds of the child cleaning up his room *after* he has played the video game are slim. Then the parent must reason with an unmotivated child (since he has already received his reward) and Dad finds himself again having been manipulated by the youngster. In this case, the child has sabotaged Grandma's rule and has actually been rewarded for his procrastination.

Now that the ground rules have been discussed, it's time to set up a behavior management system for your own home.

THE SMILEY FACE SYSTEM FOR KIDS
AGES THREE THROUGH SIX

Babies, toddlers, and most two-year-olds are not cognitively mature enough to work with a formal behavior management system. They have difficulty understanding the concepts of earning a "star" or losing a "Smiley Face" on a chart, or dealing with the rule allowing a maximum number of infractions to occur before a consequence is given. This does not mean, though, that the general behavior management techniques discussed in chapter 5 cannot be used with toddlers and young twos. Time-outs, ignoring inappropriate actions, and rewarding good behavior are behavioral techniques that can be used with even very young children. Somewhat older kids, ages three through six, not only respond to these techniques, but also thrive on formal behavior management systems involving working for rewards and avoiding negative consequences. Even if your child is too young for a formal behavioral system, mastery on your part of the basic behavioral concepts will help set the stage for success when he's two and one-half or three years of age.

If you're the parent of a child three years or older, you may have already tried star charts, Smiley Faces, or other tactics to motivate your child to do as he is told and to behave better. These programs all seem to work initially, kind of like a honeymoon effect. But when the novelty wears off, you're back to square one—threatening, nagging, and usually giving up. Kids are pros at figuring out how to get you offtrack, making you forget what you asked them to do and causing you to become inconsistent regarding consequences. So, now that we've established that kids are smart and sometimes sneaky, let's learn how to outmanipulate the manipulator by using behavior management techniques.

When I describe the behavior management program to parents, one question that usually crops up is "Doesn't this just scratch the surface and only change my kid's behavior temporarily? What about changing the attitude causing the inappropriate behavior?" It's a good question, necessitating a somewhat complex answer.

To respond, I need to talk a bit about the difference between behavioral and analytical psychologists. Behaviorists (that's me) are of the school of thought that changing the environment—mainly through the use of positive and negative consequences—changes behavior. The change can be temporary if the consequence is weak or given infrequently, or can be permanent if the consequence is meaningful and given consistently. Behaviorists also believe that if a person changes a behavior for a long-enough period of time, then the behavioral change actually leads to a change in attitude. For example, if a child is rewarded frequently for sharing her toys, sharing behavior will improve dramatically. Cooperative behavior leads to easy friendships, which in turn lead to positive self-esteem. *Voilà!*—a true attitudinal change.

On the other hand, there are some schools of analytical psychology that propose that only long-term, in-depth analysis of feelings and prior life incidents leads to true attitudinal changes (these are the "talk therapy" folks). These psychologists feel that focusing upon earlier events and analyzing one's thoughts are the keys to changing attitudes. I'm sure that many are successful with their own clients, but I've seen *very* quick results in both behavior and attitude using my behavioral techniques. Parents appreciate the practical, commonsense ideas and love the quick turnaround they see in their kids.

The second most commonly asked question is "Isn't this bribing my child to do what he should be doing just because he's part of this family?" The answer is unequivocally yes. He should be doing as told when told, as well as speaking politely to you because that's just good sense and common courtesy. But if he's not, and if we can motivate him to do these things using behavioral techniques, why not? Most folks wouldn't go to work if they didn't get paid, and many kids don't like to complete their chores without receiving something in return. Now, what they receive doesn't have to be exorbitant—it's privileges that parents usually give their kids anyway without their having to earn them. Behavior management, once you understand it, can be the most effective, humane, and simple approach to changing your child's inappropriate behaviors and attitudes.

As in many areas of life, a habit begun early is easier to establish and tends to remain longer than one started later. That's why it's important to begin a behavior management system when your kids are little. If children are expected to help put their toys away at age three, they'll be less resistant to cleaning their rooms by themselves at age eight. Four-year-olds who are given time limits in which to complete chores are more responsible later on when it comes to setting and waking up to an alarm clock by themselves when in grade school.

Quiz Time

You know that you need a behavior management system for your child if:

1. You are the parent of a child at least three years of age.
2. You've tried everything you can think of to change your kid's behavior and nothing seems to work for longer than a day or two.
3. Thoughts of shipping the child to Grandma's house (for a week, a month, perhaps longer?) are becoming obsessive.
4. You're beginning to dislike your kid even though you haven't lost one ounce of love for her.
5. You feel like a bad parent, especially after reading parenting magazines in which everyone else's kid seems to respond to the expert's suggestions.
6. You've lost control. You've turned into a nag, and this is especially frightening because you see yourself becoming more like your mother every day.

7. You now understand your parents' phrase "I only wish upon you one just like yourself."
8. You don't want to spank your child because you're afraid you'll really hurt him.
9. You feel tremendous guilt when punishing your daughter even though you know she deserves it and will probably learn a good lesson from the consequence.
10. You're still trying to "reason with the unreasonable," trying to talk your child into seeing things your way, even though the last 101 lectures didn't make a dent.

Said yes to a bunch of these? Then you're the perfect parent for a behavior management system.

The Smiley Face System

The Smiley Face system for kids three through six years of age is simple, practical, and, if you stick with it, very effective. Little ones really enjoy the structure of being on a behavioral program. They know just how far to push you and exactly what you're going to do if they go over the line!

Parents of young children tend to depend upon threats of spanking, reprimanding, and reasoning to alter their kids' behavior. We often see and hear their idle threats in the malls, at grocery stores, in restaurants, and in their homes. One of the hot spots to see little kids outmaneuvering their parents is Disney World in Orlando, Florida. Since my family lives close by, we spend many weekends at America's favorite vacation land. It's fascinating to watch pip-squeak kids totally running the show as distraught parents scramble to meet their children's needs while also taking in the sights. Lots of crying, screaming, demanding, and general kid misbehavior abound—and everyone seems to be exhausted! It's a fascinating exercise to watch out-of-control kids whose parents are placating, bribing, and hand-wringing, while spending lots of money to engage in this experience. But they all keep coming—I guess it's a rite of passage of some sort! These out-of-control behaviors are typical of the problem areas dealt with by my behavioral management system for little kids.

Setting Up the Smiley Face System

The Smiley Face system involves three Smiley Faces drawn on a sheet of paper (see chart on page 88). Each morning, one sheet is placed on the front of the refrigerator, using a magnet to hold it in place, and the remainder of the Smiley Face sheets are stored on top of the refrigerator. Each time your child behaves inappropriately, just cross out one of the Smiley Faces and write the nature of the infraction on the line under the Smiley Face. It's amazing how powerful a crossed-out Smiley is to a kid—they just can't stand it! When all three Smiley Faces have been crossed out, your child will face consequences.

But, first, let's look at typical little kid behaviors that should lead to the loss of a Smiley Face. Inappropriate behaviors for three- through six-year-olds generally center around:

* Not doing as told when told (that is, when you want him to do it, not when he decides to).
* Aggressiveness (hitting, kicking, door slamming).
* Touching things without permission (especially after you've said no many times).
* Interrupting the parent (usually while you're on the phone or attempting to talk to your spouse).
* Not taking no for an answer (bugging, nagging, and hassling you).
* Fussing and throwing temper tantrums (either verbal or the drop-on-the-floor type).

You need to individualize your kid's program to deal with any inappropriate behaviors *you* wish to decrease. Every family is different and your kid may have some especially squirrelly behaviors not listed above.

Now let's take a look at the consequences, both good and bad. Remember, you need to consistently give a consequence so that your kid knows you mean business. When all three Smiley Faces have been

SMILEY FACE CHART FOR HOME

Name: _____   Date: _____

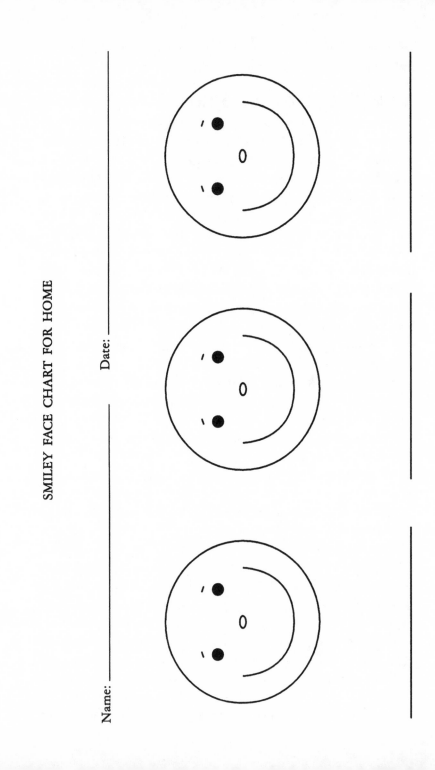

crossed out, two things will occur. First, remove one treat from a jar of four prizes that you filled for your child that morning. Treats can be candy, snacks, or small inexpensive trinkets that really turn your kids on. (Little ones love stickers, colored paper, pencils, and all that stuff.) The "lost" treat is placed back into the master bag of treats and your kid does not have the opportunity to regain that item that day. Therefore, there are now three treats remaining in the child's jar. Next comes the fun part—time-out. Your child is placed in a time-out situation as described in the preceding chapter.

This process will be continued throughout the day. Your kid's behavior is documented on the Smiley Face chart, and each time three Smiley Faces have been crossed off, the child loses one of the prizes in the jar and also spends an allotted amount of time in time-out. Upon completing each time-out, a new sheet of three Smiley Faces is placed on the refrigerator. At the end of the day (about one half hour before the child's bedtime), your child receives whatever prizes remain in the jar, if any. This is a double whammy—you're using both reward and punishment and little kids really respond to that!

A word of caution here: Very young children (three- and four-year-olds) may need to have their day divided into two parts. For instance, they may be able to earn two prizes from waking until two o'clock and then another two prizes from two o'clock until bedtime. Older children (five- and six-year-olds) can usually wait for all of their rewards until one half hour before bedtime.

I also suggest that after a long period of time (an hour or two) or a significant break in the day's activities (such as taking a nap) that a new sheet of Smiley Faces is put on the refrigerator, even if a Smiley Face or two have already been crossed out. This prevents the possibility of your child having two Smiley Faces crossed out first thing in the morning, behaving fairly well for the next two hours at the mall, and then losing one Smiley Face after lunch. This would result in three Smiley Faces being crossed out and negative consequences occurring. Too much time has intervened and the youngster may not understand why he is being put in time-out and losing a treat at that point.

These powerful parenting techniques accomplish two purposes:

They relieve you of having to listen to your child's incessant fussing. They also teach her that there is an *immediate consequence* for her inappropriate behavior. This is referred to as "response cost." Your kid has learned that fussing and crying are just not worth it. They lead to losing Smiley Faces and a treat, as well as a time-out. Sounds tough, but it works, and it certainly gets your kid's attention.

How do you know if the Smiley Face system is working? Kids tend to react intensely to this system. Most kids do very well beginning the first day since they appear to be quite attracted to the rewards and they also dislike time-out. Other kids (typically the more stubborn ones) make a valiant attempt to prove to you that the system will not work. They will go into time-out and remain there quietly, coming out only to tell you they really wanted to be in there and wouldn't mind returning. The best parental reaction, of course, would be that of nonchalance and not taking the bait.

Time-outs for losing Smileys continue throughout the day, and often these kids experience several of them a day during the first week. After six or seven days, though, even the stubborn ones begin to tire of the game and become more interested in earning the rewards. They then admit that the time-out situation was not a whole lot of fun and begin to work for the treats as well as avoiding the time-out room.

I've found this behavior management system to be extremely effective *if you are consistent*. This does not mean you should cross out a Smiley Face for every single inappropriate action—only those that are significant. (You'd be crossing out Smiley Faces all day long if you were really picky!) The kids receive the prizes remaining, if any, in the jar at the end of the day and the treats are theirs to keep. If all the treats have been lost, kids can still earn time-outs by losing three Smiley Faces. They seem to enjoy the rewards, but I've found that most kids respond to this system mainly because they dislike the time-out room so much.

Many kids need to remain on the Smiley Face system until they are old enough to be placed on a more complex home behavior management system at age seven. You may feel that you do not like having to deal with behavior management techniques and the structure of keeping a chart, but it has become apparent to me that without a behavior management system of some sort (either the Smiley Face system for little kids or a more complex system for older children), your home will become chaotic and out of control again. Even though behavior management systems can be somewhat time consuming in terms of keeping charts and Smiley Face forms, your home is run in a much more efficient and calm manner, and you'll soon find that it is well worth the trouble.

Out-of-Home Misbehavior

A note about behavior management when you're away from home. Kids have a knack for sticking it to you when you don't have a time-out room available. Many realize that and will quickly go in for the kill. Malls and restaurants are not generally conducive to time-out. However, time-out can be accomplished to some extent in a corner of the mall, but generally it is not as effective as at home, where the child can be placed in a safe yet boring spot. Also, it's really embarrassing to try to keep your kid in a corner of a store, nose to the wall. Grandmothers have a way of walking by at that point and tsk-tsking at you. Awfully humiliating!

But there is a technique that may help to keep you in charge. Try using a counter or clicker (available at most sporting goods stores) to remind you of how many inappropriate behaviors your child has accumulated while you are out. In this way, a "click" is like crossing out a Smiley, an immediate verification of your kid's inappropriate behavior. For example, if your son behaves rudely three times while shopping in the mall, you should click the counter three times and upon returning home, cross out three Smiley Faces on the chart. Then take away one of his prizes and place him in the time-out room at home. You can also use the clicker by saying to your child, "If you can keep it to two clicks or less while we are in the mall, then I will buy you a drink as we leave."

Another suggestion is to place pennies or nickels in front of a youngster when she is out to dinner with you. Remove one of the five coins when she acts inappropriately (flops on the floor, talks too loudly, uses bad manners) and the child cannot regain that coin. At the end of the meal, the child receives all the coins that are left. Usually, this is a strong incentive and a fun way for your daughter to make it successfully through a dinner experience.

These methods help you to document your child's behavior. Some kids are like junior attorneys—unless you have proof, it didn't happen! That's why clickers work so well—it's difficult to argue with hard evidence. If you try to remember how many inappropriate behaviors each child accumulated while they were on a day trip, it's almost impossible and the children will often find ways of sabotaging your memory. If you use a device such as a counter or clicker, there will be no discrepancy. (Remember—kids are always on the lookout for discrepancies to pull parents offtrack and you should be on guard for this.) In addition, just taking the counter out of your purse or pocket can often quiet a child down when he sees that you are about to use it!

Lisa

....

Our three-and-one-half-year-old daughter, Lisa, was out of control. She was wearing us out with her screaming, whining, kicking, and hitting. When Dr. Peters explained the Smiley Face system, we were skeptical that a few trinkets and treats would get her to cooperate. Were we surprised! Our daughter took a complete dislike to having Smiley Faces crossed out. She would plead with us to put up a new sheet so she wouldn't have to see those big X's. The first couple of time-outs in the completely stripped bathroom let her know that we meant business. When she finally realized we would firmly stick to the rules, she started working with us, instead of against us. The Smiley Face system helps keep us consistent, since everyone knows what to expect.

In-School Behavior

School is another environment where the Smiley Face system can come in handy. Whether your child attends preschool, kindergarten, or first grade, there's bound to be some inappropriate behavior that could use either a bit of fine-tuning or even a major overhaul.

Kids generally act up in school for two reasons: The classroom is often exciting and therefore conducive to losing self-control, and most children realize that there are very few negative consequences available for the teacher to use to punish misbehavior. And these consequences usually have very little impact: sitting for a short period in a time-out chair in the corner of the room—still in earshot and view of the activities of the other kids—or staying next to the teacher for a few minutes on the playground during recess does not have much impact. Most kids don't like these consequences, but scores of children and teachers alike have confided to me that "it's no big deal" and that kids soon become immune to these punishments.

Generally, teachers' hands are tied when it comes to disciplining their students effectively. As a last resort, the chronic misbehaver may be sent to the school director or principal. But children quickly adapt to even office visits—looking remorseful, yet returning to the classroom just as ornery as before. I've found that employing the Smiley Face system at school often works wonders with these kids. It's almost as good as having the parent there observing the child's behavior—a state of affairs that often gets the kid's attention.

If your child needs a behavioral tune-up at school, offer this program to the teacher. Have her place a sheet of paper with a total of twelve Smileys drawn on it (three rows of four Smileys per row). (See chart on page 94.) The last Smiley (Smiley number twelve) should be surrounded by a box—very noticeable and distinctive from the others. Under each Smiley (including the last one in the box), draw a line upon which the teacher can write a word or two briefly describing the child's infraction. You and the teacher should tell your child that each time she engages in any significantly inappropriate behavior, a Smiley Face will be crossed out and a description of the incident will be written on the line, so that you'll know exactly what class or playground rule was broken.

Typical school misbehaviors leading to a loss of a Smiley are:
* Not doing as told when told.
* Not taking no for an answer.
* Talking back to the teacher.

SMILEY FACE CHART FOR SCHOOL

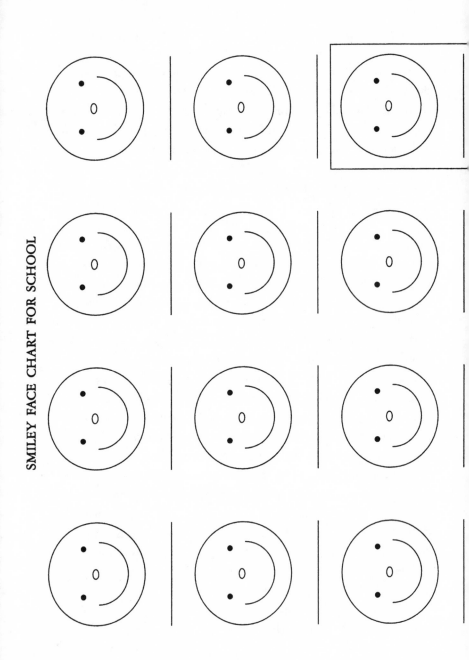

* Aggressive behavior (pushing to be first in line, shoving, biting, kicking, tripping).
* Unacceptable language.
* Not attempting or completing work.
* Out-of-seat behavior (getting up too frequently at inappropriate times).
* Talking during worktime.
* Any other behaviors that break class/school rules.

This list is described to your child in detail so it is clear to him what behaviors will result in the loss of a Smiley Face. Each day, a new Smiley Face sheet is posted in a place where it's easy for your youngster to see how he or she is doing throughout the day. If your child works at her own desk, tape a small square of paper in the left-hand corner with the twelve Smileys on it. If she doesn't have her own desk or table, pin the Smiley Face sheet to a convenient spot on the wall. The key is that the chart should always be in view so that your kid can easily keep tabs on how she is doing.

Now comes the important part—the positive and negative consequences for her behavior that day. The child is told that if she keeps the number of crossed-out Smileys to eleven or less by the end of the school day—meaning that the twelfth Smiley (the one in the box) is not crossed out—she has earned a "good day" and will receive a reward by the parent after school. If the last Smiley (the one in the box) is crossed out, then not only does she lose her reward, but she also faces a significant negative consequence at home that day.

The Smiley Face system will work at school only if four things occur:

1. The teacher accurately and fairly crosses out Smileys as the misbehavior occurs (not crossing them out all at once at the end of the school day).
2. The child is able to constantly keep tabs on how she is doing. As the twelfth Smiley approaches, she can then tone down her misbehavior.

3. The consequences (both negative and positive) are important to the child.
4. The parent is consistent with rewards for good days and punishments for bad days.

In polling my young clients and their families, certain rewards tend to pop up as possibilities: (1) stopping at a convenience store on the way home from school to get a treat; (2) earning a later bedtime at night; (3) the parent playing a board game with the child that evening; (4) an extra book read at bedtime; (5) earning a poker chip (token) in lieu of cash to be accumulated and later spent at a toy store; (6) earning a "privilege poker chip" to be saved up to earn an outing such as bowling, miniature golf, or a trip to the ice cream store; and (7) a "grab bag" treat (trinkets, crayons, glitter, etc.).

Typical negative consequences are: (1) no television, videotapes, or video games that day; (2) no outside play or friends allowed to come over; (3) early bedtime; and (4) lengthy time-out in an appropriately boring and safe location. (The length of time-out depends upon the age of the child and how stubborn she is.)

Most kids will succeed in keeping the last (boxed) Smiley intact with the threat of only one positive and one negative consequence hanging over them. However, I've met some particularly ornery kids who need to receive multiple consequences before they accept that both you and the teacher mean business!

If your child comes home the first week with eleven Smileys or less crossed out each day, then the following week's chart should contain only ten Smileys, with the last one surrounded by the box. The rules remain the same—as long as the boxed Smiley is not crossed out, your child receives the reward and avoids the negative consequence.

The goal is to reduce gradually the number of Smileys to the point where you, the teacher, and your child feel that she is sincerely trying to behave and that her previously disruptive behavior has improved and current behavior is now acceptable. Tell her that you are lowering the number of Smileys she's allowed because she is doing so well—pile on the praise so that she's proud to reduce the number of Smileys because she is behaving more appropriately.

Jack

My son, Jack, was disruptive in class, talked out loud, used inappropriate language, ran around the room, threw classroom supplies and even desks and chairs when he became very angry. He would also lash out physically at teachers and other adults in the school by hitting and kicking them when they tried to control him. Dr. Peters put him on a behavior modification program using Smiley Faces. If all the Smiley Faces were crossed out at the end of the day, he'd had a bad day. If even one was left, he'd had a good day. The Smiley Faces were backed by an immediate reward system, a sticker on the calendar, and a treat or small monetary reward at the end of the day. There was also a long-term reward if he could have eighteen good days out of the next twenty school days.

My son has responded well to this system. The small successes he achieved daily enabled him to modify his behavior enough to achieve his long-term goal. At his request, the number of crossed-off Smiley Faces allowed for the day has been decreased because he enjoys the feeling of success from achieving his goal and he now knows that he can control his behavior.

Most little kids understand and love this system. They look forward to their daily treat and often brag to their classmates about the chart. I've never seen a kid who was embarrassed by it—in fact, many teachers ask if they can use the chart with other kids who are disruptive or who are displaying inappropriate behaviors.

In this way, the teacher who previously had only a few, ineffective consequences at her disposal now has a behavioral system to use that carries with it consequences that really matter to your child.

You can use this program at school whether you employ the Smiley Face system at home or not. Consequences earned from the school Smiley Face system can occur in conjunction with those earned on the home behavior management program.

Playing Hardball

Once in a while, I run into a kid who is so stubborn that he is stoically willing to accept the "standard" negative consequences of the behavior management system without flinching. These kids continue to lose privileges such as playtime and television, as well as their daily allowance and toy poker chips.

With this type of kid I often recommend "playing hardball," which means beefing up the consequences or adding others, so that the total package becomes so intense that it just isn't worth being stubborn anymore. The child usually gives in and plays ball—and good behavior follows. So, now for some hardball ideas!

As noted earlier, time-outs begin at ten minutes, and can be lengthened by five- or ten-minute intervals as needed. It is not unusual for kids to earn time-outs for thirty, sixty, or ninety minutes, especially when they are exceptionally ornery. Some kids push the system to the point of needing time-out from the moment they get home from school until dinner, or from after dinner until bedtime. This will get any kid's attention, and they will finally give in and work with the system if they believe that they will have to face a few hours of boredom in the time-out room.

The time-out spot is also negotiable. In chapter 5, I discussed time limits and the best location for time-out, and you may want to review that section. If you find that the time-out spot you are using is not effective, you may want to consider using bathroom time-out for older kids whom you can trust to behave safely. If you do, make sure that the bathroom is well lit and ventilated and that it is safe—pills, scissors, and other potentially dangerous objects removed. Remember—boredom is one of the most powerful tools to use with your child. He will work hard to avoid it, even if it means doing things he doesn't particularly want to do.

Taking away a prized possession and donating it to the Salvation Army, Goodwill, or a shelter for underprivileged kids can often be the negative consequence that turns the tide. Many parents have tried the tactic of temporarily removing a possession that the child can get or earn back after a specified amount of time has passed or cessation of the inappropriate behavior occurs. My experience has shown me that kids are rarely fazed if they know they can get the item back. Plenty of Nintendo cartridges and bicycles are "put away" and returned within a few weeks, but the child is quite adaptable—just knowing that he'll get his stuff back eases the pain. However, realizing that he'll never see his favorite remote control car again will definitely get your son's attention, and he may think twice before talking back the next time. If he's really obstinate, it may take losing his entire collection of action figures before he caves in and watches how he speaks to you.

Many parents, however, have a philosophical conflict with giving away their kid's possessions. This stuff costs a lot of money, and they are reluctant to just give it away. When this issue comes up, I usually remind them of my hourly fee, pointing out that losing a few action figures doesn't even come close to the cost of therapy. If that doesn't sway them, I paint the picture of what life will be like with an even brattier kid if they don't get a handle on their youngster's behavior now.

Is your child a shrewd manipulator or a let's-make-a-deal negotiator? How about a don't-bother-reasoning-with-me-because-I'm-unreasonable child? These types of kids often need consequences that are creative and perhaps go beyond the traditional ones. For instance, the rule of "one minute of time-out for each year of age" just doesn't work. Now this may be fine for fussy kids one through three years of age, but from age four on, it's a whole new ball game. Putting an extremely willful four-year-old in time-out for only four minutes is usually a waste of four minutes and accomplishes very little. Many of the brattier preschoolers I work with do not respond (their behavior does not improve after the consequence is given) until the timer is set for at least ten or fifteen minutes. I've also worked with lots of four- and five-year-olds who needed thirty to sixty minutes of an *effective* time-out situation (not playing with the dog in the bedroom) before it hits home and they change their behavior.

You'll know that you're getting close to hitting pay dirt when you say something like "If you don't clean up your toys before the timer goes off, then you will lose your last Smiley Face, and go into a ten-minute time-out in the guest bedroom. And I'm going to have to close the door because in the past you kept coming out." If your child actually moves and cleans up the mess without an argument, you know that your disciplinary system is becoming effective.

It's an awesome feeling when that happens. "Yes! All right! I've got control again!" But it can also be somewhat bittersweet. You may have conflicting feelings such as "This is great, what a super kid, I'm a brilliant mom" along with "What? I had to use a longer time-out to control my own child and I needed a book to tell me it's okay to use a longer time-out?" But you'll feel better, you'll like yourself and your kid much more, and you can spend the newfound time doing positive, fun things with your child rather than constantly yelling and nagging.

Let's look at another means of playing hardball—the controversial disciplinary tactic of spanking. I have to tell you that, personally, I'm not thrilled with hitting anything—kids, pets, spouses, etc. I believe that there are usually smarter, more effective ways of changing someone else's inappropriate or rude behaviors. However, as I've said, I have met many families over the years who swear by spankings. These folks tell me that if they have already stated a rule and the child has purposely (not unintentionally) broken it, that a swat on the butt makes the point and the behavior decreases or even ceases. I've heard it from enough responsible, loving parents that I have to believe that in certain controlled situations, spankings (or the threat of them) can be helpful.

The things to consider before spanking are:
1. Have your tried all of the nonphysical consequences first, and have they proved ineffective? If not, try something else before using corporal punishment.
2. Is this the only form of discipline to use if you're stuck in an inconvenient location (such as a restaurant or the middle of the mall)? If not, try to get to a time-out location.
3. Can you personally live with the emotions following spanking

your child and can you feel comfortable doing so? If not, don't do it.

4. Is your temperament calm and stable enough so that you can give a truly "controlled" spank, one that is not given in rage? If the answer is no, then don't hit the kid.

5. Does your child really respond to controlled spankings? If not, don't do this to yourself or to your child.

What is "controlled spanking"? Sounds like an oxymoron to me—something like "a fascinating math test." A controlled spank means that you are hitting your kid, but doing so in a controlled manner. The child is warned of what is about to occur and why (told once, not lectured). The placement of the spank is always and only on the kid's buttocks or the fatty rear of the legs, or possibly the hands or fingers of a toddler who constantly reaches for dangerous items (hot pans, scissors, etc.). *The spank is never to the face.* I've met innumerable kids whose parents have intended to smack their cheek, but the child moved his head suddenly and the open hand landed on the ear, causing the eardrum to break. (Think about living with that guilt for the rest of your life!) Also, cool off before you spank. You may decide that a different, more creative approach will work better. Spanking in rage will lead only to bitter, resentful, and hateful feelings on the part of your child, feelings that you will probably have to deal with for a long time to come.

Also, kids who are hit too often tend to become immune to it. Even controlled spankings can lose their effectiveness if it's your mainstay of discipline. I suggest that if you choose to keep spanking in your bag of disciplinary tools, that you save it for those times when the consequences discussed earlier can't be used, such as when you are out of the house and time-outs are tough to do, a privilege taken away doesn't seem to matter to the child, or you need to instantly gain your kid's attention.

As noted, I've met many parents who report good results with controlled spanking. I've seen their kids, who tell me that they know their boundaries, that their folks mean business, and that the spanking was deserved. It's the kids who report that their fathers or mothers "lose it" and spank in a rage who get to me. That's abuse, and there's no other word for it.

So, think about this issue. Are you a "capricious spanker," falling out of your usual mode of overtolerance of negative behavior (in which you take lots of junk from your kids) only to finally let loose and wallop them? Children of capricious spankers report to me that they are often afraid of their folks (and not afraid in the healthy way I spoke of earlier in chapter 3), because they can never really predict what will push their parents' buttons. Other kids play the odds—accepting the 80 percent chance that Mom will do nothing makes up for the 20 percent of the time that she freaks out and cleans their clock.

When considering using spanking as a disciplinary tactic, ask yourself how you felt about your own folks' use of corporal punishment—the inveterate spanker often mimics the parenting style that he endured as a child, and since he obeyed his parents (out of great fear), he hopes also that his kids will obey. One problem with this is that you may still experience remnants of bitter feelings toward your own folks, and you have to decide if you want your kids to follow suit.

If you decide to include spanking in your disciplinary program, think it through very carefully. Be sure your spouse accepts spanking, because it will lead to many a marital battle if the two of you disagree (your spouse doesn't have to use corporal punishment with the children, she or he just has to agree that you can under certain circumstances).

Decide when, why, and how spankings will be delivered. Be sure that other nonphysical options have been tried first, or are difficult to use at the time. And, finally, if you swat your kids, do so only if it works. Many parents hit out of frustration, not out of expectancy of success. And keep it to a minimum. If you're hitting your child more frequently than before, it's obviously not working. You may feel immediate vindication and that you've "let off some steam," but I can guarantee that random, uncontrolled, ineffective smacking will come back to haunt you for years to come as you try to bond with a child who is bitter and resentful toward you. That just doesn't seem worth it to me.

7

BEHAVIOR MANAGEMENT FOR DEVELOPMENTAL ISSUES

J ust as challenging as dealing with inappropriate behaviors, maintenance issues of child development can unnerve even the most patient of parents. I'm referring to such daily activities as finishing meals, using the potty instead of the diaper, and sleeping in one's own bed. Let's start with sleeping, as it is the earliest problem to emerge of the three (the other issues are rarely dealt with before toddlerhood).

Sleep Problems

There is not much that you can do about your child's sleeping habits as a newborn, except to pray a lot. Some babies sleep five or six hours the first night home from the hospital, whereas others are up every ninety minutes or so, demanding to be held, diapered, or fed. Some wake up for seemingly no good reason at all—they're just up, and so are you! If your neighbor has a newborn who sleeps six hours right from the start, envy would be an appropriate emotion to have. Her good fortune probably has not so much to do with how she treats the baby—she's just lucky. Most of us have to endure between six and twelve weeks (sometimes even longer) of extreme sleep deprivation before Junior settles in and gives us a break.

My philosophy about kid sleep behavior is that there really are no right or wrong answers—just end results. Every family is different and has different expectations and tolerance levels. If you don't mind getting up throughout the night with a baby or having your three-year-old sleep in your bed every night, then you probably don't need the tactics described below. But if you'd like to get some sleep and keep the parental bed "adults only," you may want to try some of the following suggestions.

Although the newborn's sleep cycle is fairly set by his own biological clock, there are some things that you can do to encourage longer sleeping periods as he matures, as well as sleeping more at night than during the day. First, try to stick to a nap/sleep schedule as much as possible. This may mean waking the baby in the morning so that he will be more amenable to taking his nap on time as the day progresses. It's tempting to let him sleep, but you'll probably pay for it later as his sleep schedule is thrown off and he's still bright-eyed at midnight.

Second, have an established routine whenever you put the baby down in the crib. Perhaps feed him first, then change the diaper and soothe him in a way he likes. Try to put him in the crib before he falls asleep. If you don't, he may not be able to fall asleep anywhere but in your arms—which can be very inconvenient when your second child arrives and you find that you can't hold both of them at the same time.

Third, try to stick to a routine in other areas of your life. If possible, do your errands around the baby's schedule so that he won't miss too many naps and become overtired. Most parents have experienced the enigma of the exhausted baby—she may be so beat that she just can't fall asleep. If this occurs, sometimes the only thing that works is to take the baby for a ride in the car—the motion and noise will usually knock her out.

Okay. Now the kid is asleep, it's 11:00 P.M., and you and your spouse have just gone to bed. Rustling noises from the intercom suggest that either your baby is just moving around and getting comfortable, or perhaps you're in for a long night of howling. If the noise evolves into whimpering and crying, give it a minute. Many babies will find a way to calm themselves back to sleep if you just let them try it first. Give your baby the chance to learn to handle falling back to sleep herself. This is called "self-calming." If you continue to hold her and take the responsibility for "making her fall asleep," she'll take longer to learn to do it herself. However, if after only three or four minutes, the baby is *howling,* it's probably time for one of you—hopefully, you're taking turns—to change the diaper and try to calm the child back to sleep.

William Sammons, writing for *Child*, discusses self-calming. "The emphasis in self-calming is on self . . . the baby settles herself down without assistance from anyone. As her ability to self-calm improves, a child can prevent herself from getting upset in situations where she used to cry. Eventually she can use these skills to gain more self-control and begin to entertain herself. . . . Babies who self-calm sleep longer, nap more predictably, feed more consistently, and are socially more responsive."

At four months of age, if your child is still depending upon you to get her back to sleep after a quick check and diaper change, it may be time for you to "bite the bullet" and let the baby have a few nights of crying it out and learning to fall back to sleep herself. Most of the time, babies recover from this much more quickly than do their parents. While you're still wallowing in guilt, your child is probably thinking some baby version of "Oh, they must mean business now." It's amazing, but I believe that even kids as young as four months of age can force you to take responsibility for their sleep habits and will continue to wake throughout the night as long as they know you'll give attention and cuddle them. (I advocate lots of cuddles and kisses, but 1:00 A.M. may not be the appropriate time.)

The issues surrounding teaching baby to sleep in his crib and to calm himself are fertile ground for producing enormous guilt in parents. It may help if you try to think like a kid: "If I scream, they pick me up, give me attention, and calm me down." Sounds logical, but it keeps the parent exhausted, as well as depriving the child of learning one of his first lessons in self-control.

However, let's suppose that you've succumbed to the cries and for two and one-half years you've participated in your child falling asleep in your bed and staying there all night. When it's only occasional, sleeping together as a family can be kind of nice—sort of a group bonding experience. There's really nothing sweeter than waking up in the morning with a kid snoozing near your face. However, when he's with you almost every night, it gets real old, real fast. Besides the lack of privacy, kids have a way of taking up well over their third of the bed and landing punches even as they sleep.

If your child has become a nightly visitor, or even a permanent resident, and you want to change this (remember, the choice is yours—there are no definite rights or wrongs about your child sleeping in your bed), I suggest using a behavior management system to keep her out of your bed and in hers. First, if she has developed the habit of falling asleep in your bed, encourage her to lie down in her own at bedtime. If necessary, after the bedtime ritual has been completed (taking the bath, brushing teeth, reading a book to her), sit in a chair near her bed (not in the bed) while reading your own book to yourself silently. Tell her that you are not going to engage in conversation since she is to be asleep soon. Some parents keep a jar of five candy or token treats handy, and every time the child talks, they remove one—or, better yet, eat the candy themselves, so the child realizes that not only is she going to be ignored, but she actually loses one of her treats in the process. In the morning, give her all the treats that are left in the jar from the night before as a reward for going to bed and staying there.

Eventually, she'll learn to quiet down and, after a few nights, may cease trying to engage the parent in conversation. Once the child is quiet, the odds are greater that she will fall asleep. Some families play tapes of soothing music to relax their kids, while others try to keep this time as quiet as possible. Some keep the room dark, while other kids prefer halogen floodlights—do whatever works!

Once she is sleeping, leave the room quietly. If she wakes during the night, have a sleeping bag and pillow ready for her on the floor of your bedroom near your bed. Tell her earlier in the evening that if she wakes up and can't go back to sleep in her own bed, it's okay to come to your room but *not to get in your bed and not to wake you up*.

She won't like this at first because the sleeping bag on the floor is not nearly as comfortable as your bed, but remind her that if she does wake you up, she'll be marched back to her own room and she can scream it out there. Usually, just a few times forcing the child to remain in her room does the trick, especially if she realizes that she actually has the option of coming into your room as long as she sleeps on the sleeping bag and does not wake you up.

So, if you want to take control of your kid's sleep problems, I suggest adopting the following rules and consequences:

* A special treat is given in the morning for making it through the night in her own bed.
* Neither negative nor positive consequences are given if she comes into your room in the middle of the night, sleeps on the sleeping bag, and does not wake you up.
* A negative consequence such as loss of playtime or TV/videos the next day is given if she wakes you up or climbs into your bed. Of course, if your child is sick at night and needs your help, she is encouraged to seek you out. This distinction should be made clear to her so she won't be afraid to get you if she is actually ill.

Michael

....

*M*ichael was nine months old and still not sleeping through the night. He was our first child and we always had an excuse to rock him back to sleep. We were all waking up exhausted each morning and knew something had to be done, especially since we were expecting our second child in three months. We decided to let Michael "cry it out." After a couple of nights of "giving in" after he cried for two straight hours, we decided to give it one more time. Little did we know that we were about to experience the most bizarre and torturing weeks of our lives. We placed him in his crib at 8:00 P.M. and there he sat—upright, staring at the door—for eleven hours of straight crying. He lost his voice after about seven hours, but he still tried his best to cry. I kept telling myself that if we gave in, we'd never change his behavior and that it would be almost impossible to do it with a newborn coming in a few months. As the sun rose, Michael was still crying, staring at the door, sitting upright in his crib with his head bobbing from exhaustion. We put him to bed the next night only to find him still determined not to lie down and go to sleep. He sat up crying for two hours until he finally collapsed forward onto his ankles. I gently placed him on his side so he could breathe.

Then a strange sleeping pattern developed. He would now fall asleep, but he wouldn't lie down. We'd find him sound asleep sitting up, his head bobbing. When we tried to sneak in to place him on his side, he would wake up again. I was ready to go back to the rocking so he could sleep more comfortably. He seemed to be getting enough sleep, but we did not know if he would ever learn that it would be comfortable to lie down. This went on for another week. Then, one night, like a miracle, he just lay down and slept. He's been doing it ever since.

Mealtime Wars

After sleep problems, the second most common maintenance issue that I hear about are children's fussy eating styles. Most babies do fine when breast or bottle feeding. Milk and formula are bland and the baby soon adjusts to the taste and consistency of the liquid.

Many pediatricians recommend beginning with "starter" foods (soft substances with the consistency of thick formula such as rice cereal or applesauce) around baby's sixth month. Other doctors suggest waiting several more months before introducing foods, which may help to avoid predisposing the child to food allergies.

Most of us have videos or photos of our little one's puckered-up face as he first experiences the various consistencies of different foods. Not only are the tastes new, but kids are not quite sure what to do with the food. It seems that no matter what they try, their tongues get in the way of swallowing! However, after some practice, Junior eventually figures out how to chew and swallow to get the darn stuff down.

Many babies and toddlers seem to enjoy bland cereals and fruits but have trouble accepting vegetables and meats. Part of the difficulty is due to the coarse consistency of meat and veggies, but also many kids just don't like the taste. As kids evolve through the stages of development, they experience the taste of the same food differently. For example, a salty French fry may be rejected at an early age whereas it may be craved as the child's taste for salt develops. Many parents have described their toddlers as "grazers"—trying most foods put on their plate—only to become very picky eaters by age four or five. I explain that the pickle may have tasted great at three years of age but is perceived as disgusting at age five. So not all eating problems are based in the child's fussiness or trying to be difficult—sometimes kids are merely not ready for certain foods or have "outgrown" the taste for them. Also, consider the baby in the high chair who has little choice of what to eat. Mom shoves in a spoonful of pureed green peas and there isn't much baby can do about it. If his tongue pushes it out of his mouth, Mom masterfully scoops it up and shoves it back in. Might as well give in and swallow, under those conditions! However, the older toddler has learned how to spit, lock his jaw like a clamp, bite the hand that feeds him, and throw food—all good defenses when someone is trying to con him into eating mushy green stuff.

The smart parent, though, realizes that due to the child's changing perception of taste as well as escalating defenses against "yucky foods," mealtimes may become more difficult. You need to become creative and try to prepare foods that look appealing to the child, have the taste and consistency he enjoys, as well as to capitalize on his increasing independence in order to encourage better eating. Many two- and three-year-olds will eat finger foods (cut-up hot dogs, baby carrot sticks, Cheerios) not only because they like the taste, but also because they can play with the food and exact some control over the eating situation.

Most pediatricians are opposed to force-feeding children, since this often leads to habitual battles at the dinner table as they grow older. Studies have shown that, given choices, most kids will, over a period of time, take in the necessary vitamins and minerals that they need for good health. (Remember, this is over a time period. Therefore, the child may choose to eat mostly fruits one day or carbohydrates another, but will ingest a proper diet if allowed to make some of his own choices.)

Now, not many of us have the time, patience, or personality to allow Junior to select his own meals every day. However, we can use this knowledge to relax a little, knowing that if our child doesn't eat well for a day or two, it's usually nothing to worry about. And if the child receives a daily multiple vitamin, it adds insurance.

Another common food mistake made by many parents is failure to realize how little food many kids actually need to eat at each meal. Two tablespoons of peas, four or five bites of chicken, and a piece of bread are usually plenty for a four-year-old's lunch. However, parents tend to think like adults and view such a meal as a mere snack or appetizer. Little kids' stomachs are small and therefore quickly relay to their brains that they are full.

Kids like to eat several small meals (or snacks) a day, rather than the three large ones that most adults prefer. This is because the appetite center in the child's brain is working efficiently. The brain lets the child know when she is physiologically hungry (needing more glucose in the blood to fuel the body) and only then will the child desire to eat. When her body sends a message to the brain's appetite center signaling that it is "full" (enough fuel has been taken in), she'll stop eating.

That's the way nature has wired most animals—it's adaptive and healthy. Rarely do you see an overweight animal living in the wild— usually only house pets and people overeat. Even predatory sharks follow this rule, eating only enough to feel full, then not again until the brain's appetite center signals that it's time to start looking for another meal. That's how sharks can coexist in aquariums filled with lots of yummy little fish. Rarely do they eat their aquarium mates, since they are fed every other day (the natural appetite cycle of the shark) by the aquarium biologists.

Not only are food fights with our kids unnecessary and unwarranted, constant forcing of kids to "clean their plates" (and therefore eat more than they need or want) only teaches the child to ingest more food than is necessary. Over the years, the youngster will learn to ignore the sensations sent out by the brain's appetite center and to eat because food is available, not because she's really hungry. As many of us adults have come to realize, this is the very behavior that leads to obesity, afflicting over one-third of adult Americans.

So, as long as your pediatrician feels that your child is healthy (although he may look awfully skinny to you), take the lead from your kid as to how much he needs to eat, how often, and what foods he enjoys most. Introduce new foods as he grows older, and reintroduce some that he rejected a year ago—he may like them now as his taste buds have matured.

Some families use dessert as a reward for eating a "good dinner" or employ some other type of consequence. If you do, I would suggest using dessert as follows: "No dessert unless you have tried what is on your plate. If you try it and really don't like it, let's find something else you do like to eat. If you're still hungry for dessert after you've finished, then you can have some." Offer the dessert, but don't push it on the child.

Some folks force their kids to sit at the table for hours because they refuse to eat or taste a particular food. Personally, I wouldn't eat something that I'd been looking at for half an hour—it probably is cold and tastes awful! It's best to avoid this frustrating trap by setting a time limit to determine when the meal is over. Kids who are hungry will have finished and dawdlers will be set free but will not receive dessert.

Mealtime wars are just not worth it. Often they lead to control battles that nobody wins. Generally, kids will eat well if their portions are small enough and you've taken into consideration their individual likes and dislikes. You'd probably like your kids to remember you for the good times, not for the battles over broccoli.

Potty Training

Potty training is a rite of passage—often the delineation between toddlerhood and becoming a preschooler. Most parents prefer to let their child "tell" them when she is ready to give up the diaper, but some folks find themselves in the unenviable position of having to rush potty training in order to meet criteria for admission to a preschool situation.

Some preschools take the humane approach of helping to train the child by having him watch his peers use the potty, whereas other facilities adhere to a firm "no diaper" policy. If the preschool of your choice insists upon the latter, you certainly have a challenge, especially if you have only a short amount of time in which to accomplish this goal.

We have all heard of someone's kid who virtually trained herself—just woke up one morning, ripped off the diaper, plopped her butt on the potty seat, and, *voilà!*, mission accomplished! However, for most parents, potty training is usually a trial-and-error event—initially beginning at twenty-four months, trying again at thirty months, and if unsuccessful, finally succeeding at three or three and one-half years of age.

As the personalities of children differ, so do maturity and readiness for potty training. Some kids don't want to be bothered—they have spent their entire lives peeing and pooping in their diapers, are used to the sights and smells, and could probably go a few more years with Mom or Dad doing all the work. These kids are the ones who have to be convinced that there is something in it for them in order to go along with the potty-training program.

Others are eager to lose the diaper and don pull-on disposables or training pants. These tend to be independent kids who are modeling their behavior on older children in their families or play groups. They consider pottying a fun and interesting activity and take great pride in their accomplishment.

A third type of kid, probably the most frustrating, is the child who appears to be trained but is consistently inconsistent—on one week, off the next. The parent knows that the child understands what is expected of him and also feels that he is developmentally mature enough to control urinary and rectal muscles. He seems to lose interest, though, and frequently has relapses.

Let's take a look at what works best for each of these kids. First, the child who couldn't care less. Louis, at two and one-half years, seemed to have absolutely no interest in learning how to use the toilet. An only child, he had no older sibs to model after, even though his father, Paul, toileted with him in an effort to interest him in how big boys behave. Paul had been determined to train him by his second birthday, mainly because his mother told him he was trained at sixteen months, even though that's highly unlikely. But Grandma stuck to her story and Paul felt pressured to push Louis's potty behavior.

Paul bought his son a toddler potty, and Louis would easily comply and sit on it. But after a minute or two, Louis had enough of sitting and was up and running around, either diapered or still bare-bottomed. Shelly, Paul's wife, didn't buy into the pressure from her mother-in-law and urged her husband to relax and to back off. She believed that Louis would be trained when he was ready. Shelly was able to stay home with Louis, so she also felt no need to hurry the process in order to get the child into a preschool program.

Paul gave in for a little while, but when Louis was twenty-eight months, he started trying to interest the child again. This time, Louis cried when placed on the potty and even began to hide in the corner of the room when he pooped in his diaper.

Instead of backing off, Paul showed his disappointment by telling Louis that he was a "baby" since he still wore diapers. To a toddler, being called a "baby" is like hearing a four-letter word. Louis became angry and began to bite his own arm when Dad started in.

By two and one-half years, Shelly had had enough and brought the family to my office to help straighten this out. When I talked to the child about pottying, he avoided the subject by losing eye contact and playing with the buttons on his shirt. However, when I asked him about his beloved teddy bear, he was able to hold a pretty good conversation for a little kid. Obviously, Louis had become traumatized by the potty-training experience and avoided dealing with it whenever he could.

I suggested that *everyone* needed a break from this issue and insisted upon a one-month hiatus in which potty behavior was not addressed at all. Pull-ons were to be used instead of diapers so that Louis could get used to the feel of them, but Mom and Dad still did the changing.

I saw the family after the month had passed and set them up on a positive reward schedule. We used a "successive approximation approach" (gradual steps to goal achievement). First, Louis was rewarded just for taking his pull-on down when being changed. He was given his choice of rewards—either a sticker, a colorful stamp on his hand, or a few M&Ms. Louis tended to switch off between rewards and soon asked to be changed frequently because he wanted to win a treat.

The next step involved taking his pull-on off by himself (stepping out of it) before he was given a reward. After that was accomplished (which took only a few days), Louis was told that to get the treat he had to take off his pull-on and to sit on the potty. He chose to sit backward on the toilet, holding on to the tank lid for security. He used a child's step stool to climb up on to the toilet and one parent was always with him to make sure that he didn't fall in (it's very scary to slip into the toilet—lots of kids do it. They may prefer to use a child's toilet seat cover or a child-size potty instead). Louis was rewarded for sitting on the potty for just one minute, and then the time was increased to two, three, and four minutes before he received a treat, even if he didn't urinate during that time. His parents put a tape recorder in the bathroom and Louis listened to songs while he waited. If he didn't whine or fuss during this time, he received a treat as well as a gold star posted on a chart on the bathroom wall. When he had earned ten stars, Louis could pick out a nice treat from a goody bag his folks had put together for him (filled with little cars, blocks, and crayons).

In the meantime, Shelly had arranged for Louis's four-year-old cousin, Jonathan, to spend time at their home a few days a week. Jonathan, already potty trained, allowed Louis to observe his toileting behavior, as he was told that he was helping to teach his younger cousin how to use the bathroom. Jonathan was pleased to do this, especially when he learned that he would receive a prize for "going" also. After a few weeks of this regimen, Louis was very comfortable undressing himself and sitting up to five minutes on the potty—but, still, nothing was happening. At a therapy session, I told him that from then on, he would receive his treat and star only if he urinated in the toilet, as he had seen Jonathan do. He didn't seem very happy with the new arrangement but was told that it was his choice—to get a reward, he had to urinate in the toilet. Meanwhile, Jonathan was racking up the stars and M&Ms!

At first, Louis tested the waters—sitting on the toilet and asking for a star without urinating. But Paul and Shelly remained consistent, telling him to let them know when he had urinated and that only then would he be rewarded. Also, Jonathan was growing richer by the day. At long last, after five days of holding out and urinating in his pull-on, Louis peed—in the toilet! You'd think the kid had won the Pulitzer by the way they carried on. Shelly, who had witnessed the event, immediately called Paul, and Jonathan clapped and shouted.

After that, it was a piece of cake. Louis peed in the potty six or seven times a day in order to win the prizes and stars, as well as to be congratulated by his parents. After a few weeks, he was rewarded only once a day with a larger prize if he didn't wet his pants that day, instead of a star and small prize for each pottying incident. By Louis's third birthday, he was trained during the day and also was using the toilet for defecating. He didn't become dry at night until later, but Paul and Shelly could live with that.

Louis is an example of a child who is not naturally interested in the pottying process and had been pressured too early into dealing with a behavior he was not ready for. With the use of rewards and role modeling by his cousin Jonathan, Louis gained interest and became successful.

The second type of child I spoke of, the one who is curious, independent, and virtually self-trains, is a pleasure. If your kid seems to fit into this group, one of the best ways to complete the process is to let her run around the house bare-bottomed for several days, so that getting on the potty is easy and quick and accidents are avoided. Once she has this down to a science, training pants or pull-ons can be used. Pile on the praise—she's not only pleasing herself, she's pleasing you and loves your hugs and kisses for being such a "big girl."

Be prepared, though, for a few months of "emergencies" as your daughter gives you no more than a five-second warning in the mall in which to find a bathroom, because she "has to go!" (and now!). As she develops, she'll begin to notice the physiological urges preceding urinating or defecating and will be able to give you more notice.

Nighttime may still necessitate a pull-on, but soon she'll awaken at the feeling of urgency and go to the bathroom herself.

Now for the kids who specialize in giving you gray hairs: those who absolutely, positively have been trained for weeks at a time but have relapses on a regular basis.

These kids seem to do well in structured situations, pottying when you keep them on a schedule by sending them to the bathroom thirty minutes after a meal or upon returning home from school. If left to their own devices, however, they tend to become distracted. Stopping play to take the time to use the bathroom just doesn't seem important, and they can easily play with wet, even poopy pants.

I've found that teaming rewards with punishments works best for this type of kid. Each day that the underwear is dry deserves a reward—possibly a token for an arcade game, a star on a chart, a small treat, or a poker chip to be accumulated to be traded in for a trip to the toy store at a later date. In addition to the reward, the negative consequence of having to clean her own underwear will usually have an impact on your child. Most of these kids can sit in wet pants, but don't like to touch them with their hands. Have her wash them out in the tub or sink, and then place them in the washing machine. She'll soon realize that ignoring the urge and wetting her pants is just not worth it, and she'll do a better job getting to a bathroom on time.

Pottying can be a struggle—it's often one of the child's first attempts at not only controlling his bodily functions, but also showing you who is boss. It's best not to even play the control game because he'll probably win. Use a behavioral technique that forces the child to choose between taking responsibility and thus earning the reward, or being irresponsible and facing a negative consequence. Showing your frustration only seems to make her more stubborn, determined not to give in to your demand to dispose of the diaper routine.

So now your child is urinating in the potty, dry during the day and perhaps even at night. But he refuses to poop in the toilet. He may hold his stool until you put a diaper on him in order to poop, or he squats in the corner and poops in his pants. (I've had several young clients who use this method regularly—and they even take off the dirty underwear and hide them under the bed. Not a pleasant discovery on cleaning day!)

What to do? First, be sure that your child is physiologically healthy (have the pediatrician do a quick check) in order to decide whether she is ready to be potty trained for defecation. If you feel that she's either just being ornery or is afraid to poop in the potty, then you can try the following method.

I call it the "bare-butt" technique and it usually works well. Tell your daughter that from now on when she's home that she'll be wearing only an oversized T-shirt with no shorts or underwear on underneath. When she has to poop she is to use the toilet or child-size potty, but she cannot put a diaper or pull-up on (you may have to hide them and use them only for nighttime).

I've never had a kid that would poop on themselves without a diaper or pants on. I can't explain it, and no child has ever been able to tell me why. But they just don't seem to like the sensation of poop sliding down their legs or sitting on it later. Finally, they will concede to using the toilet, especially if you have offered a treat for each poop in the potty.

Allen

....

We have three children, and our middle son, Allen, encountered some difficulties when the time came to be toilet trained. Dr. Peters explained to us that Allen was indeed a strong-willed child who at four-and-a-half years of age was using toilet training as a control issue with us. She recommended that over the next weekend we take away Allen's pants and underwear during the day and let him wear a long T-shirt that would cover his lower body. We explained to him that should he have the urge to go to the bathroom, he would be ready for it, but that he could not wear diapers any longer. We were obviously concerned about not appearing cruel or humiliating him and we made sure his brothers would not make fun of him.

He felt very uncomfortable and would not even sit anywhere. However, on the second day, he came to us and said he would go to the bathroom on his own and would never soil his pants again if we agreed to give him his underwear back. We said he would have to prove to us several times that he was toilet trained before we could give him his privilege back. During the whole time, we were very affectionate to him and reassured him of our love for him, but we held on to the system even when he begged. By the fourth day, we trusted he was ready to get his pants back and he never soiled his underwear again after that.

Therefore, to avoid potty problems:

* Wait until your child is old enough to begin training. Do not believe your mother that you were trained at sixteen months— you probably weren't, and if you were, you've most likely paid for it psychologically in some way.

* By age two and one-half most kids are developmentally ready and have enough muscular control to feel the urge and to get to the bathroom in time to urinate. Many are ready by two years of age, but you should treat your kid as an individual. If you're being pressured by a preschool that insists that two-year-olds be out of diapers, find another facility or licensed day care home where your child can gradually begin the process.

* If your child shows initiative and interest, go for it! Heap on the praise as she tries out sitting on the potty. Work with her to see if she prefers sitting forward with her feet on a stool, backward holding on to the tank lid, or prefers a child-size training potty.

* Use lots of rewards for success. I guarantee that you will not have to continue to give out prizes and stars for potty behavior at age fourteen! Little kids need this reinforcement and respond well to visual reinforcers such as a star chart, as well as food and trinkets that reinforce how well they are doing.

* Use a potty-trained buddy, relative, or older sibling as a model for correct potty behavior. Kids often learn quicker from each other's behavior than from adult suggestion.

* Relax! To my knowledge, no one has ever left for college in diapers!

Dr. Marianne Neifert, in her astute *Parenting* magazine article "It's Potty Time!," suggests the following seven rules when considering potty training your child:

1. Look for readiness signs, such as your child being able to understand and follow simple requests—he's able to walk to the potty and sit on it by himself, shows evidence that urination is about to occur, can verbalize the need to go to the bathroom, and stays dry for at least two hours at a time.

2. Use anatomically correct names for body parts. "When an elbow is an elbow, but a penis is a weener, children wonder why one part of their body is so special that it can't be called by its real name," writes Neifert. Also find out the bathroom lingo used at your child's day care situation so that he can clearly communicate his needs to the caretaker.

3. Make sure that you have all the necessary equipment, including a comfortable potty chair, pull-ons or training pants, easy-on-and-off clothing, and a book or video about potty training.

4. Go slowly. Wait until your child is comfortable with removing his own pants and sitting on the potty before requesting him to be able to jump right in there and sit long enough to be successful.

5. Take it one step at a time. Begin by understanding your child's idiosyncratic signs that he has to urinate or defecate (it's usually quite obvious) and expect daytime dryness before nighttime success.

6. Encourage all caretakers (parents, grandparents, baby-sitters) to be consistent. All need to be on the same wavelength so that the child gets the message that self-pottying is an expectation, not a game to be played inconsistently.

7. Assume that accidents will happen. It takes a while for the child to be able to tell that his bladder is filling up. At first, kids don't seem to notice until it's an emergency and you have no lead time to make it to the bathroom. Also, most children hate to

stop their play to take a potty break—they would rather continue building blocks than interrupt their fun. Initially, these kids need to be reminded every hour to try to go to the potty. After a while, they can perform the whole process so quickly that it barely interrupts their playtime.

8
BEHAVIOR MANAGEMENT FOR SOCIAL AND EMOTIONAL HEALTH

The behavior management programs presented in chapters 6 and 7 focus upon typical child behaviors that tend to drive parents nuts. However, use of behavior management techniques is not limited to changing socially inappropriate behaviors or dealing with maintenance issues. Almost any inappropriate or ineffective behavior can be modified using this system. Many parents have brought kids in to see me for specific behaviors that, at first glance, would seem likely to respond only to traditional talk therapy and not be conducive to a behavior management approach. These may be emotional or social issues, or even personality problems, but I've found that many behavioral, social, and personality problems can be solved if treated with behavior management techniques. Let's take a look at two of these more common child emotional problems from a behavioral perspective.

Cheering the Miserable Wallower

Even emotional areas that were once thought of as problems amenable only to extensive talk therapy have been found to be appropriate for behavioral techniques. One of these, the miserable wallower, is exemplified by six-year-old Matthew.

Matthew appeared to his parents, Ray and Clare, to be a chronically negative kid. When a group of children came over to play and a spat developed, Matthew would huff out of the room and pout, stating that nobody liked him. If he lost at Nintendo, he declared that he wasn't good at anything. Matthew spent much of his time appearing sad, complaining, and feeling sorry for himself, and his worried parents became concerned for his emotional health. They mentioned it to his pediatrician, who referred the family to me for an evaluation to rule out childhood depression.

I interviewed Ray and Clare first and it was interesting how differently they each perceived the situation. Clare, being somewhat of a "marshmallow mom," worried constantly that Matthew might grow to be suicidal if he continued his pessimistic attitude. She would spend hours listening to his negative self-statements, trying to talk him into seeing things in a more positive way. But Ray, who had initially reacted like Clare, had tired of Matthew's grumping and had actually begun to avoid his son, as Matthew's negative manner irritated his father.

The next session was with Matthew alone and I quickly saw how his dad could become annoyed by Matthew's excessive negativity. Even good things were tainted with the possibility of gloom! Matthew always appeared to be waiting for the other shoe to drop, and in the meantime, he couldn't enjoy the neat things that were going on in his life.

Matthew had become what I call a miserable wallower, someone who chronically seeks out what is or could go wrong in any situation and then begins to brood and complain. This had become a habit for Matthew. He had fallen into the rut of perceiving the world in a negative way. His parents had reinforced this attitude by fretting over his sadness and trying to talk him out of his negative self-statements. Instead of ignoring self-criticism, they had actually been rewarding him for talking and acting as if he were miserable, and therefore Matthew had become miserable.

When I met with Matthew and his folks at the third session, I described this style of behavior and how Matthew was actually most comfortable when he was grumpy. Acting miserable had become a habit pattern for him and he saw nothing wrong with dumping his bad moods onto his family, even if it worried or irritated them. In his own way, Matthew was manipulating his folks. They chose vacations around what would irritate him the least, and bent over backward to make sure that they gave him lots of attention when he seemed down.

I suggested that they try an experiment with Matthew and respond to his negativism differently from the ways they had in the past. Instead of rewarding Matthew with sympathy and attention, his parents needed to either ignore his negative self-statements or reward him with praise, encouragement, or even a treat when he chose to see the bright side of things. Matthew seemed uncomfortable with this suggestion, but his parents committed to following it to help their son become happier with himself.

The program worked well. After three weeks, Matthew's self-statements were generally positive and he seemed to be happier. He could still be moody, but Matthew actually liked the rewards he earned for his new positive attitude, and chose to let go of much of his old negativism.

Kids who appear miserable may be miserable—they can be very unhappy, lonely, and even suicidal. I always take them at their word until I evaluate what emotions truly lie behind their statements. If they are really depressed, a referral to a psychiatrist may be appropriate. However, if I feel that this emotion is based more in a pattern of having become comfortable with misery, I quickly move to a behavioral approach to reduce the negative self-statements.

Differentiating between true depression and the habit of being miserable can be tricky, and the diagnosis should be made by a counselor who is familiar with the symptoms of each. True depression is associated with definite behavioral signs, such as changes in sleeping and eating patterns and social withdrawal. The miserable wallower usually doesn't display these characteristics, but tends to show a pattern of negativism following disappointments. If you're not sure which it is, check with your pediatrician for referral to a competent counselor who can make the diagnosis and recommend the most beneficial treatment.

Once the habitual negative statements are lessened, it is much easier to gauge what is really going on in the child's life to better deal with it. In essence, this program shows the kid that he is not allowed to act miserable unless he truly is, and most of the time I find that children are not truly sad—they may be angry or defensive or just wallowing in old habits. Use of a behavior management approach, therefore, is definitely something to consider before labeling your child as depressed and resorting to medication or other intensive treatments.

Conquering Fears and Phobias

One of the most common emotional traps children encounter as they mature is experiencing fears and phobias. Baby fears tend to focus upon strangers, loud noises, and separation from parents. Toddlers may cringe at the sight of large dogs or even a frisky cat whose quick movements are unpredictable. Fear of the pediatrician is common, since your little one may feel a bit manhandled as the doctor checks every orifice and gives inoculations.

As the child approaches the two-and-one-half-year mark, it may seem that your heretofore macho man has suddenly become very cautious in some areas. Your young Houdini who previously escaped from his crib and could be found roaming the house in the middle of the night now at age three insists on lights in his bedroom and is afraid to go to the bathroom alone at night. What's different? Cognitive maturity, that's all! Your son has reached the point in his development at which he is able to understand danger and to be afraid of it (he's experienced enough cuts and bruises to connect walking in the dark with banging into the wall).

From three to six years, the fears can blossom to cover almost every aspect of the child's life—bogeymen and monsters take up residence in closets and under beds, lovable stuffed animals look menacing in a darkened bedroom, and scary movie or television characters visit your child at night for weeks or even months at a time.

What to do? First, realize that fears are normal. Few kids escape childhood without having to deal with some intense anxieties. Be supportive. Never belittle your youngster for being afraid. Although *you* know that all that's under the bed are dirty clothes and broken toys, *she's* absolutely, positively sure that there's at least one monster lurking below. Many parents lessen the anxiety by performing the nightly ritual of checking the closet and looking under the bed before turning out the light. If this becomes a habit, so be it—it sure beats having your kid frightened and sleeping in bed with you every night! If your son insists upon bright lights in his room at bedtime, try using a lamp with a dimmer switch, which can be purchased inexpensively at most hardware stores. Over several weeks' time, slowly lower the amount of light produced so that your child doesn't notice the difference. You can even change the lightbulb over time to a lower wattage (without his knowledge) as he becomes used to going to sleep with less light.

By respecting your child's fears, he will not feel bad about himself—he'll see the fears as challenges to overcome, not as threats to his self-esteem. I often tell my young clients that I still can't watch scary movies because I'm positive that the creature will end up under my bed that evening! By letting kids know that their fears are not only normal but that you may have experienced some of the same ones as a kid yourself, the shame is lessened and they are more willing to try to overcome the fears if they do not feel humiliated. Also, make sure that older siblings do not make fun of the youngster for his fears. I realize that this is fertile ground for teasing, but it should be made clear to the provocateurs that this issue is totally off limits and negative consequences will occur if they even begin to go there.

If the fear does not naturally dissipate over time and becomes either a significant burden to the family or the child, therapeutic measures may need to be taken. Six-year-old Mark had the fear of going into his bedroom alone after dusk. This reticence to visit the bedroom had been tolerated by his folks for years. Mark's toys were moved to the family room, he dressed in his parents' bathroom, and he slept with them every night.

Once he began first grade, though, Mark's fears began to stop him from enjoying some important activities that many six-year-olds experience. He was afraid to sleep over at friends' houses, he stayed up too late at night waiting for a parent to go to bed with him, and when kids came over to play, they commented on how weird it was that

Mark's bedroom was almost empty of toys. He began to feel ashamed and depressed.

Mark's parents, Sandy and Dennis, had been ultimately too patient with their son. They had very little privacy themselves and felt that they were at his beck and call when they had to escort him to his bedroom at night every time he needed something from it. Since Dennis traveled a great deal, the bulk of the nightly routine fell upon Sandy. By the time she and Mark came to my office for counseling, Sandy had begun to lose patience and Mark was feeling conflicted—he wanted more than anything to be rid of his fears, but was worried that his mother was going to force him into the situation cold turkey.

I recommended using a system of *successive approximations* in order to slowly help Mark conquer his fear of being in the bedroom alone at night. Together, we set up a list of scenarios, ranging from some that were only slightly scary (such as Mark entering his room with Sandy standing in the doorway) all the way to Mark going to his room alone at night, putting on his pajamas, and sleeping in his own bed. Just the thought of the latter frightened him, and I could tell we were going to have to progress slowly through the stages of Mark conquering his fears step-by-step.

I suggested that we reward him for successful completion of each step by using poker chips and baseball trading cards (which he loved). Upon successful completion of his nightly "homework assignment," Mark received two baseball cards and a poker chip (to be saved to later trade in for a toy or an outing). Mark was enticed by the rewards and wanted to begin the program that very evening.

It turned out that Sandy was not only motivated to lick this problem, but that she also was very creative! She easily developed ten stages of progressively more anxiety-producing situations. At first, Mark was rewarded each night for just running to his room and bringing back an object to his mother, proving that he had done it. Later stages involved Mark finding notes his mother had written earlier and placed on his desk, with instructions for him to do a certain activity while alone in his room at night. For example, Mark would have to write three spelling words five times each on the small blackboard hanging on his wall before he was able to dash back to the safety of his parents to receive his rewards. Before too long, Mark was spending evenings in his room, and eventually sleeping the night in his own bed.

Sandy and Mark made this a creative, fun experience, and although the "homework assignments" were somewhat anxiety-producing at times, Mark took great pride in accomplishing each stage, as well as enjoying the rewards of the poker chips and baseball trading cards. The program was so successful that they generalized it to Mark's walking alone to the neighbor's house and back at night (under Sandy's watchful eye from her front door). Mark also began having friends over to spend the night, as well as sleeping at their homes.

Not only did Mark learn to overcome the specific fear that brought him to my office, but he also learned another very important lesson—how to work to overcome obstacles in life. His folks were proud of him, but more important, he felt terrific about himself.

Nelson

*M*y son, Nelson, is six years old and an only child. He is afraid of many things, but one of the saddest things is that he was even afraid in our home. Once it became dusk, he was afraid to go to his room. It became such an issue of frustration for my husband and me that we sought help with Dr. Peters. She was able to find Nelson's "comfort zone." It helped when it was raining outside (because who would be out in the rain?), or if he had the dog in the room with him or music lightly playing, or the air conditioner running when he went to sleep. They were all good distractions, but our goal was to have Nelson go to his room after dark to get ready for bed without one of us standing there and constantly checking on him. Dr. Peters told us to try various "games" to make him go to his room and, eventually, keep him there by himself. I would have him retrieve certain items for me—say, five in a row, so he would have to make five trips. Then we had him stay in the room for a count of ten, then twenty. We had him solve a puzzle I would put on his blackboard, such as unscrambling words or hangman. Gradually, he progressed *so much that by the end of six months, he was going away for a weekend sleepaway at his church camp! You can imagine the concerns we had, but when he came home, he was so proud of himself—while the other campers waited, he had walked back into his dark cabin by himself one night to pick up his thermos!*

As you can see, fears and phobias are common occurrences in childhood. In fact, it's the unusual kid who doesn't have some difficulties in this area. Dr. Mark Rubenstein provides the following list of common fears that emerge in childhood and when to expect each one.

Infants	Toddlers	Preschool	School Age
Strangers	Separation	Monsters	School
Separation	Toilets	Animals	Bullies
Noises	Noises	Bedtime	Teachers
Falling	Bedtime	Day care	Tests
	Day care	School	Getting lost

So, if your child is concerned with the bogeyman, sleeping alone in a darkened room, or large dogs, don't be too upset. Most of this he'll outgrow, especially if you are supportive and patient with him.

Self-Esteem and Leadership

When I speak with parents about their goals and dreams for their children, two of the most common themes are good self-esteem and leadership ability. Parents value both of these in themselves and their peers and therefore try to set the stage for their own children to develop these same qualities.

First, let's take a look at self-esteem. Literally, the word connotes how highly one respects oneself. Often, self-esteem is based in the security of knowing that you are well liked, competent, and successful in your interactions with others.

What can you do as a parent to reinforce good self-esteem in your child? The answer is conceptually simple, but may be difficult to carry out. Accomplishment and success involve facing challenges (be it stacking blocks, learning to ride a two-wheeler, or memorizing the alphabet). And challenges generally involve frustration. (If the new task isn't frustrating, it probably won't be a challenge!) The parent's job is to allow the child to deal with challenges by himself, to face frustration, and to learn self-control in order to persevere, even if the going gets tough. The time to step in, though, is when you see that the youngster is in over his head, offtrack, or becoming so frustrated that no amount of self-control or perseverance will lead to success. That's when you need to help with the puzzle piece, hold the bottom two blocks so that the third and fourth ones can stay on, or suggest to the novice bike rider that she call it a day and try again tomorrow.

Parents' tendencies to step over the line between helping the child to succeed and actually performing the task for them can, over time, send a negative message to the youngster: "You can't accomplish this—let me do it for you." Of course, that's not what the parent sets out to do, but it's often how the child interprets it. Kids need to experience a few emotional and physical bumps and bruises—it's the best way to learn about life and what works and what doesn't. By overprotecting your youngster, you're actually preventing these learning opportunities and the child may grow up to feel inadequate and insecure.

It's also important to heap on the praise and encouragement when deserved, and to watch that your constructive comments are not easily misinterpreted as negative criticism. This is especially important if your kid tends to have a defensive nature, interpreting *all* comments as negative.

Other areas of competency that are important to the development of good self-esteem are social and academic. Getting along with peers at preschool, grade school, and on the playground plays a powerful role in how kids ultimately feel about themselves. If they are rejected, most kids come to blame themselves and to feel that there is something wrong with them. Observe your child at school and at play. If she is behaving socially inappropriately (acting too aggressively on the playground, calling out in class, or shying away from others), bring this to her attention so that she'll begin to understand the effects her behaviors have on others. Try to teach her to be tuned in to how others perceive her, and suggest ways in which she can be seen as a better friend, a more interesting person, or someone who's just easy to play with.

If athleticism appears to be a ticket to good self-esteem in your kid's play group, try to help your son develop his motor skills by playing ball with him, teaching balance by practicing on a balance beam, or just playing chase in the yard. The more he runs, the faster he'll go. The better your daughter is at jumping rope, the higher esteem she'll receive on the playground from her peers. Remember, kids have a pecking order very similar to that of adults—those who accomplish more than others tend to be held in higher regard. Whether this is fair or not is irrelevant—accomplishment appears to be a distinctly powerful basis for acceptance by others, leading to your child's enhanced self-esteem.

And don't forget academics. Kids who can call out the alphabet at least at the same rate as their peers feel comfortable in the kindergarten classroom. Those whose letter and number knowledge is shaky begin to feel poorly about themselves and either act out to cover up their self-doubts or withdraw and pretend to be invisible. That's why it's important to keep up with the Joneses in this area—it's tough on a kid who is placed in a classroom with others who actually learned kindergarten work in pre-K. So if you believe in taking academics slowly, that's fine, just be sure that your child's classmates are on the same level and that the school's academic philosophy coincides with yours.

Encouraging Leadership

When I interview parents, I often ask for a list of their kid's positive attributes as well as the problem areas that have brought them to my office for therapy. One of the most common positives I hear is that their child is a leader—not always taking the other kids down the right path, mind you, but at least charismatic enough to be able to persuade others to follow along. Rarely do I hear folks bragging that their kid is a "good follower." In our culture, it seems that leading is to be applauded and the rest of us are assigned the second-rate role of following the chosen one.

Personally, I believe that the world is capable of handling only so many leaders, and that good followers (as opposed to resentful "leader wannabes") are what really make up the backbone of society. Be that as it may, leaders really do get the limelight—more teacher attention, greater peer respect, and more scholarships to college. So let's take a look at promoting leadership ability in your youngster.

There are two types of leadership roles available to your child—that of the *social facilitator* and that of the *idea generator*. The former is more popular with the preschool set, but in grade school, the idea generator often begins to emerge on the most-wanted list.

First, let's take a look at the social facilitator. These kids appear to be born leaders. Early on, they know how to work a crowd—they make good eye contact, are animated and humorous, and take teasing well. Marcy, a four-year-old I was seeing due to her parents' recent divorce, was such a leader. She was a magnet even for new kids she met at the park. Within a few minutes after bounding out of her dad's car, Marcy would be leading a troop of followers up and over the play gym as well as directing the games. This was one self-confident young lady, able to be decisive and displaying the uncanny ability to motivate kids to play games that both she and others liked. Marcy was a happy, extroverted child who not only knew how to handle others, but truly enjoyed the responsibilities of the leadership role. Her father was pleased that the recent divorce had not upset her true nature and he encouraged Marcy's outgoing ways.

Another of my clients, six-year-old Stephanie, had a different leadership style. She was an idea generator—much less flashy than Marcy, but just as much a leader. Stephanie's strength was in creating a multitude of ways to tackle a problem, be it on the playground (how four kids could equitably share three sand toys), in the classroom (how to get the work done more quickly so there would be extra time to use the play centers), or at home (how to make a closet double as an igloo).

Stephanie's leadership style is as important as Marcy's, albeit more subtle, and just as attractive to others. Although extroversion has often been thought of as mandatory for leadership, the quiet idea generator is often as respected for her creativity and ability to achieve goals.

It's interesting to note that leadership tends to go hand in hand with birth order. Twenty-three of the first twenty-five United States astronauts on space missions were either firstborn or only children, as are the majority of American presidents. Why? Probably because firstborn and only children tend to be exposed to more adult behavior than are their younger siblings, suggesting that the quality and amount of parental time spent doing and talking with your kids sets them up with the confidence and knowledge that are respected by their peers.

Other factors that have been found to promote leadership ability (both the social facilitator and the idea generator types) are:

* Time spent playing with others and therefore learning how to resolve the inevitable conflicts,
* Helping introverted kids gain confidence in skill areas so that they become proficient in idea-generating behavior,
* Promoting your child's self-expression so that he can clearly get his ideas across to his peers,
* Teaching your kid frustration tolerance skills so that he comes to view problems as challenges rather than as obstacles,
* Promoting perseverance (few follow a leader who quits easily),
* The ability to share the limelight—the basketball star who passes the ball to the teammate closest to the basket is applauded by others because they can count on him to put the needs of the group (winning the game) above his own personal desires (making the basket himself).

All these skills are appropriate to work on with all kids regardless of whether yours is destined to be a social facilitator, an idea generator, or a good follower.

9

BEHAVIOR MANAGEMENT FOR SOCIALLY INAPPROPRIATE BEHAVIORS

I n chapters 6, 7, and 8, I focused upon various behavior, maintenance, and emotional problems typical of children under the age of seven. These situations covered the bulk of problem behaviors displayed by kids in this age group—mainly, noncompliance and the challenges inherent in growing up and taking responsibility for oneself. However, several specific issues, generally in the area of socially inappropriate behavior, continue to crop up and cause problems for the parent or the child. Behavior management techniques can effectively and efficiently be used to modify these areas also. Let's take a look at some of these in depth.

Socially inappropriate behaviors are displayed by almost all toddlers and little kids to some extent. Not every child engages in all of them, but at one time or another, either you or your child's teacher will have to deal with some of them. The hit list includes:

* Aggression
* Biting
* Not sharing
* Bossiness
* Lying and stealing
* Temper tantrums

As the child enters his second year, parents come to expect episodes of biting, emotional meltdowns, aggression (hitting and pushing), bossiness, the inability to share, and a little lying and stealing. These are all normal behaviors for preschoolers but can be exacerbated when the children have not been taught appropriate alternative behaviors, or have not consistently received negative consequences for negative actions. (You'd be amazed at the self-control available to youngsters who have been taught alternatives to socially inappropriate actions.) Let's take a look at aggression first.

Aggression at School

"Use your words, not your hands" is usually rule number one at preschool. Teachers encourage kids to come to them if someone is teasing, bossing, or bothering them. Even when hitting or pushing is discouraged as retaliation, a child's first instinct, when annoyed by a peer, is often to lash out at the offender. It's almost a reflexive act, but one that can be modified if the child is consistently placed in time-out or loses a privilege for his aggression.

With some children a few minutes in the thinking chair will work, but with strong-willed kids, it usually doesn't get the job done. With the latter type of youngster, I suggest either using a longer time-out, missing out on an activity, such as center time, or sitting on the bench during the playground period. If these consequences alone fail to be effective, using the Smiley Face system at school should work. (See chart, page 94.) For instance, if too many Smileys have been crossed out for inappropriate behavior on the child's chart at school (displayed where the youngster can easily keep track of how he's doing during the day), the parent may choose to give a negative consequence at home (since a significant consequence usually cannot be given during the school day by the teacher).

This consequence can take the form of an extended time-out at home, the loss of a possession (given away, not put away), and/or the loss of a privilege or early bedtime. Too often parents and teachers think that children cannot connect their behavior at school with a consequence (either negative or positive) given hours later at home. However, I have found just the opposite to be true. Even three-year-olds are capable of understanding this system, and with the visual aid of the Smiley Face chart to remind them constantly of how they're doing, they can control their behavior in school because they know that either a negative or a positive consequence will occur later at home that day.

The combination of teaching kids alternatives for misbehavior, coupled with meaningful consequences (positive for good behavior and negative for inappropriate actions), teaches the youngster self-control as well as good decision making. To me, this is as important as teaching academics, since later success depends greatly upon getting along with others, persevering, and displaying self-control. In fact, it helps with academics since self-control goes hand in hand with concentration.

Aggression at Home

Most kids fight with their siblings—I believe it to be the sport of childhood. Although no one enjoys getting beaten to a pulp, most will endure some pushing and shoving for three reasons. First, fighting can be fun—letting loose emotions that have been pent up is a great tension reliever, and parents often witness a certain calm after the sibling storm. Second, fighting breaks up the boredom, and to most kids boredom is a horrible state of affairs. The trouble is that what begins as playful wrestling or verbal jousting can often escalate beyond the fun zone and become nasty. Third, sibling fights usually lead to parental attention. It's difficult for parents to ignore wails, screams, and loud insults coming from the next room. Inevitably, we rush in to check it out and end up playing judge and jury, a job most of us could do without.

In sibling battles, both kids *always* see the issue differently. The kid to draw first blood claims that he was provoked, while the seeming victim claims innocence. The smart parent quickly learns that getting involved is futile and finds ways to stay out of the war zone. It's interesting that the majority of my clients claim that their kids rarely report fighting when a parent is not in earshot. They swear that the kids battle for the attention of their folks! To best avoid this no-win situation, try using the Smiley Face system. The rule is that *anyone* involved in a tiff (either verbal or physical) immediately loses a Smiley. Most of the time that means that both kids lose one. If the fuss continues and all three Smileys get crossed out, both lose a treat and go to separate time-out rooms. Once the kids realize that fighting results only in negative consequences (and not parental attention), the frequency of sibling battles often decreases significantly.

Biting

Another socially inappropriate behavior typical of little kids is that of biting. About 20 percent of children engage in biting behaviors at one time or another in their kid careers. Parents tell me that they usually react by reprimands, spanks, soap in the mouth, and even biting the child back. Each to his own, but I don't think that I'd recommend the latter!

I've come up with a consequence that's easy to use, humane, and, best of all, works. After receiving your pediatrician's okay, buy a purse-sized breath spray (one without alcohol in the formula) and give a spritz on the tongue when he bites. Because the taste buds of little kids are still quite immature, the taste and odor of the spray is quite noxious to them. One or two spritzes usually does the trick. The heretofore biter thinks twice before nipping again. Talk about making the punishment fit the crime! Remember, kids learn quickly. Often after only one experience of this negative consequence, their biting behavior usually decreases or ceases.

Not Sharing

Learning to share is a prosocial behavior that is one of the last developmental roadblocks to be conquered. Babies to twelve months of age appear to share well—they're easily distracted, so when one toy is taken by a peer, another toy can be quickly switched for the original with hardly a howl. However, the toddler soon learns that if something is taken away from him he may not get it back, and that just won't be tolerated! Ever notice that preschools tend to have several sets of the favorite toys, such as blocks and ride-ons, so that squabbles are held down to a minimum? They've learned that by this age, kids realize when a treasured toy's been taken away and a fight may ensue.

If you would like to promote a greater sharing attitude in your child, try using a behavior management approach. Sit with your child as he plays with a friend or two. Reward each kid as they either offer a toy to another or fuss only minimally when a toy is taken from them. Verbal praise (including hugs and kisses), a colorful stamp on the hand, a sticker, or an M&M all work great. Smart kids will soon be giving away even your stuff to their friends just to receive a reward!

However, if your child's favorite toy or stuffed animal is involved, watch out. All bets may be off when it comes to sharing special treasures. Savvy parents put away the most important possessions when the play group is at their home. Why set the kid up for failure? After all, there's only so much sharing any child can endure!

When siblings fight over the same toy, it may be a good idea to warn them that you will remove it for a while if they can't work it out between themselves. If they can't stop battling, take the toy away for a few days. When it's returned, set up a schedule for each child to use it, and be sure to stick with it.

In some families, Nintendo wars become so vicious that the set must be removed permanently or a second one given as a birthday or other present. The bottom line is that if your kids don't share well and fight over objects, you don't have to tolerate it. Do something about it. Since you can't get rid of the kid, the possession may have to go. Your children may be unhappy at first, but they will have learned an important lesson—when you say *enough*, you mean it.

Bossiness

There's a not so subtle difference between standing up for one's self and being bossy. Righting a wrong in an appropriate way (for example, your child not allowing his peer to butt in front of him in line) is an acceptable action. But pushing others out of the way, constantly demanding the full attention of the class, or insisting on playing only his choice of games are obnoxious behaviors. And that's exactly what many kids think of their bossy peers—that they are obnoxious. Often parents of bossy children perceive their youngsters as strong. "No one is going to get one over on my Johnny," Dad proudly proclaims. Well, not many people are going to like him, either.

Bossy kids are often raised by a bossy parent. Your child's best teacher is the adult in the home. If you are loud, abusive, or demanding, most likely your child will be, also. How else is he to learn how to treat others than by mimicking his "teacher"? So, if you're trying to decrease your child's tendency to boss others, take a look at your own behavior first and change it if necessary.

Next, watch your child in play with one or two peers. Prearrange with him that when he's nice and allows others to lead or to make decisions, you'll place an M&M or token (to be accumulated and cashed in at a later time for a treat) into a jar. Bossy or selfish behavior, on the other hand, will result in removal of one or two tokens or candies from the same jar. Your child (and perhaps his friends) will receive all the treats left in the jar at the end of the play period. Concomitantly, use verbal praise when any of the kids allow the others to make decisions. And you may want to offer alternatives if they come to a standoff. "Pick a number and the one closest to the number I'm thinking of will go first this time and last the next time." Such a simple idea, but many kids never think of it.

Supervising, rewarding, and giving suggestions during one play period probably won't make a dent in your child's bossy nature. You'll have to schedule these sessions several times, but practice usually pays off. As you can see, I'm not suggesting just that you reprimand for bossy behavior, I'm encouraging you to couple giving positive and negative consequences with the teaching of prosocial alternatives.

Lying and Stealing

As the child reaches his fourth birthday, a wonderful cognitive process develops (what psychologists call symbolic functioning). This type of thought process includes magical thinking ("Step on a crack and you'll break your mother's back") and imagination (the Lego castle becomes a kingdom and your child is the ruler of all).

The positive side of evolving into this stage of development is that your kid becomes an even more interesting creature—developing play worlds in which he conquers the bogeyman and learns to control his fears while exploring safely and creatively from the security of his own bedroom or play area. This is a normal stage of development for four- and five-year-olds—one that should not only be accepted but encouraged by parents. The downside of all this is that some kids misuse their newfound creativity and imaginative powers, resulting in inappropriate behaviors such as lying, cheating, and taking things that don't belong to them (both objects and ideas).

First, let's take a look at lying. Most kids lie for one of two reasons. The most common is an attempt to avoid having to do a chore that is either inconvenient or uninteresting. If your daughter says that she has made her bed but really hasn't, she's attempting to avoid the task, hoping that you won't check up on her. If she gets away with it often enough, lying may become a habit, since she is rewarded for not telling the truth. If you *consistently* check to see what's been accomplished, most likely she won't bother to continue lying, since it will only double her burden. Not only will she have to go back and complete the chore, but will also receive a punishment for not telling the truth.

The second most common kid reason for lying is the child's attempt to avoid taking responsibility for breaking a rule or damaging something. I love the story of the mom who became concerned because her four-year-old daughter was too quiet while alone in the living room. When Mom called out her name, the child quickly answered, "I wasn't playing with your glass angel collection, it wasn't me!" even though her mother had not even mentioned the angels!

Call it what you want—lying, fibbing, engaging in white lies, making up stories, fudging, and, don't forget, omitting—all are normal but socially inappropriate behaviors that many kids engage in during this stage of development. They do so in an attempt to either get out of work or to avoid punishment for misbehavior, reasons that are not particularly nice but are understandable.

If your kid takes a few excursions into this area, that's okay. Hopefully, he'll receive negative consequences and learn that lying is just not worth it and decrease or cease this behavior. If left unchecked, many children will continue to lie throughout their lives because they feel it works for them. These kids are actually being rewarded for not telling the truth. As I noted in chapter 5 regarding behavior management ground rules, human nature is such that rewarded behaviors continue to occur and those that are given a negative consequence usually decrease or cease.

To tackle this problem, I suggest pairing the negative consequence for lying with a *brief* discussion of how you feel when your kid doesn't tell the truth—trust is decreased and you will not be able to allow certain privileges in the future if you can't believe that he will do what he says he will (for example, letting him take responsibility for turning off the light and going to bed himself after reading his book). Let him know that you understand his reasons for lying, perhaps even that you tried this behavior out yourself when you were a kid, but found that it just wasn't worth it.

The key to stopping lying before it becomes a pattern is to react calmly and to give an effective consequence. Be careful not to overreact. Your attention may actually encourage this behavior or cause your child to dig in his heels and commit to proving you wrong, adding lie upon lie. Give the consequence, lecture briefly, and move on.

Stealing consists of two possibilities: taking other people's ideas (such as copying schoolwork or cheating on a test) or taking their things (either borrowing without permission or actually stealing). Many two- and young three-year-olds assume a "whatever is yours is mine" attitude and often just take whatever they like (even though they have great difficulty with sharing or giving away their own stuff). I don't label this behavior as stealing; young children just haven't learned the boundary between your belongings and theirs, which you need to teach once they get older. Children three through six years of age can be taught limits by consistently taking away the object, returning it to the rightful owner, and explaining to the child why taking others' belongings is inappropriate. Thickheaded kids may also need a negative consequence to occur if you're sure that they understand the concept but remain doggedly determined to abscond with others' possessions. I've found that one of the best ways to handle the stubborn thief is to not only take back the stolen possession, but also to make her give away one of her items as well. She'll soon realize that she's engaging in risky behavior and it's just not worth it. As always, consistency is key—if she gets away with it more times than not, stealing behavior may continue because it seems to pay off.

The savvy parent of the sneaky kid may also choose to lower temptation by putting away enticing items such as money, special treats, or jewelry. "Out of sight, out of mind" usually works, and lessens the odds that your would-be junior burglar will even begin this behavior.

As for taking others' ideas, when your child enters grade school, he will be faced with work that is challenging, and he might meet a kid or two who is "spooky smart"—someone who effortlessly colors within the lines, cuts accurately with scissors, and can name all seven continents. Not only are these kids bright, but their academic prowess may be downright annoying and intimidating to many of their classmates. Most children can take these wonder kids in stride—either respecting, envying, or ignoring them. But some children (usually those who are insecure or overly competitive in nature) become quite jealous or intimidated, and are obsessed with one-upping these children. Some resolve to work harder, and if they perceive that their end product is still deficient, may cheat and use the wonder kid's ideas, or actually take his work and try to pass it off as their own. Less-driven children may not try to compete, they just guess at the answers and hope for the best.

I've found that kindergartners and first graders who engage in these behaviors respond well to a frank discussion of their behavior. Why do they feel the need to cheat rather than doing the work themselves? Are they lazy, disorganized, and unprepared, or do they feel that no matter how hard they try they won't succeed?

Let your child know that by using others' work, he's cheating only himself. Take this opportunity to discuss values, responsibility, perseverance, and the fact that not everybody has the same strengths and weaknesses. If he's a perfectionist, there's no time like the present to show him that less than perfect is fine. In fact, perfectionist people are often chronically dissatisfied and unhappy. The goal is to learn to work to his potential, not to over- or underachieve. Kids need to learn a balanced lifestyle and this training can begin in the early grade-school years.

Temper Tantrums

Most kids tantrum, some more than others, and this behavior takes many forms. The flop-on-the-floor head banger is sure to get attention from his audience, as is the kid who performs a screaming meltdown when frustrated. Then there's the arm biter (preferably his own), the kid who throws everything in his reach, and the quiet (but equally aggravating) pouter. All of these children have different tantrum styles, but the basis for the behavior is the same. "I'm frustrated and I won't put up with it. Do something about it now or I'll keep throwing a fit!"

Some tantrums are based in the child's inability to succeed at a task—the four-year-old becomes frustrated when she can't keep the crayon between the lines or the fourteen-month-old has trouble reaching high enough to get what she wants from a shelf. Other tantrums are sparked by an adult not giving the child what she desires—a cookie before dinner, a toy at the mall, or permission to stay up later to watch television. In any case, the bottom line is frustration, and kids don't do that emotion very well. And they will continue to display a low tolerance for frustration if they aren't taught by parents and teachers to take no for an answer, to keep trying until the crayon stays within the lines, or to compromise and try an easier piece of work instead of beating their head against the wall trying to do something that's just too difficult. Too often, however, in our effort to please our children, to make life easier for them, or to avoid hassles, we give in to tantrums. This, of course, actually rewards the inappropriate behavior and will most likely lead to more of it.

Using the Smiley Face system can stop a tantrum in its tracks. Cross out a Smiley when Junior starts to blow. If the loss of a Smiley causes louder screaming, cross out another one. If he continues, mark out a third one, send him to time-out, and remove one of his treats from the jar. If you are consistent, he'll tone down the frequency and loudness of his meltdowns as he tries to avoid time-out as well as other negative consequences.

Samantha

*F*or as long as I can remember, my youngest daughter, Samantha, who is five and one-half, has been more difficult than most children her age. When I say difficult, I am referring to sudden outbursts when she transforms from a sweet, friendly, cooperative angel to an angry, demanding, controlling handful. My husband and I tried endless time-outs, giving choices, the occasional spanking, and locking her in her room. Nothing worked and we went to see Dr. Peters. We were advised not to single out Samantha as the problem, but instead to have the whole family involved in a new discipline/reward system. This really put us at ease, since we didn't want to label Samantha as the "problem child."

We implemented a reward-based token economy in our home, using the Smiley Face system, time-outs, poker chips for earning rewards, and, finally, timers to remind her that she is performing a task and cannot dawdle or wander off. This system has been in our home for four weeks now and the change in both my daughters' behavior is amazing. Instead of yelling and getting nowhere, Samantha now knows what behavior is unacceptable and expects to lose a Smiley Face when she is out of control. She hates time-outs in the bathroom, but she goes without complaining because she knows she deserves it. The time-outs have become fewer and fewer because she doesn't want to lose any of her treats. I even overheard her one day telling her cousin to hurry up and put on her shoes because she wanted to beat the buzzer. She proceeded to tell her how boring it was to go into time-out. It was obvious that this was working. Now some of our friends call asking me for the details on how this works, because their children have asked if they can do it, too!

Tantrumming toddlers who are too young to understand the Smiley Face system may need a different tactic. Try ignoring, distracting, or giving moderate comforting—sometimes these will work. If not, time-out in a safe place, such as a playpen under your watchful eye, may break the anger of the moment. The main message to be sent, though, is that tantrums will not be rewarded, they will be ignored or a negative consequence will be given.

BEHAVIOR MANAGEMENT FOR CHILDREN WITH ATTENTION DEFICIT DISORDER

Attention deficit disorder (ADD, also known as attention deficit/hyperactivity disorder, or ADHD) appears to have become the "designer disability" of the 1990s. ADD is characterized by poor attention skills, impulsivity, and in some cases hyperactivity. You may be wondering, "But aren't most little kids, especially boys, simply like that?" The answer is yes. Lots of twos, threes, fours, and some five-year-olds have a tough time with self-control. It's not unusual to visit a preschool class and notice many of the girls quietly playing in the dress-up center or cooperatively building blocks together, while the boys are running around, talking loudly, or even out of control. However, by the time the child enters kindergarten, he should be able to sit relatively calmly in the circle line and listen to the teacher read a short book or give instructions. He should also be able to focus on starting and completing a task.

If your active five-year-old seems to be maturing and becoming less impulsive, it's often best to wait a few months before jumping to the conclusion that he has attention deficit disorder. By midyear, if his teacher is still concerned that he is not learning effectively, then it may be appropriate to consider an evaluation to rule out attention deficit disorder.

A very large percentage of parents who come to my office have been referred by school guidance counselors, teachers, and pediatricians to determine whether their child is experiencing true attention deficit disorder, or whether the kid's inappropriate actions are based in a controllable behavioral problem. Often I find that if behavior management techniques are employed both at home and at school, the child's actions improve. Then it is obvious that ADD was not the problem, as the behavior really stemmed from poor behavioral habits leading to a lack of self-control. To determine proper treatment, it's important to distinguish the noncompliant behavior of the youngster with attention deficit disorder from the willful misbehavior of a kid with a conduct problem, such as the power-hungry tyrant or the if-then kid discussed in chapter 4.

Willfully noncompliant children can clearly control their behavior if motivated to do so, whereas the youngster with ADD may not be able to consistently comply, especially in overstimulating or chaotic environments. Sequential instructions such as "turn off the TV, pick up your toys, and brush your teeth" may need to be broken down into smaller components, since the ADD child may forget some of the requested tasks. Punishing the youngster for noncompliance if he has actually forgotten the request is not fair. That's why I usually begin treatment with a behavior management program in order to determine if the child's behavior can be controlled if he is motivated and able to do so.

Parents are easily frustrated by ADD kids since many of these children experience abrupt mood swings in addition to their impulsivity, inattention, and noncompliance. Teachers often do not know how to handle ADD kids, especially those who are hyperactive. Without early identification and proper treatment, the consequences of ADD can be serious—depression, conduct disorder, and, most important, school failure. A psychological evaluation is often necessary to determine whether your child has true ADD or whether the disorganization and noncompliance are due to learned behavioral problems. Your pediatrician is a good place to start in order to get a proper referral for evaluation.

Depending upon the source, the statistics for the number of school-age children with attention deficit disorder range from 3 to 5 percent

(Ch.A.D.D.) to 10 to 12 percent of boys aged six to fourteen (United Nations International Narcotics Control Board). Medications are often used for the treatment of ADD, the most common being Ritalin, a psychostimulant. The use of methylphenidate (Ritalin and its generic versions) has increased 60 percent from 1993 to 1995, leading the United Nations' International Narcotics Control Board to warn that this drug may be overprescribed, especially in the United States.

Previously, pediatricians and child care workers felt that ADD disappeared at puberty. We now know that many of the symptoms continue well into adulthood for 30 to 70 percent of the people diagnosed. These adults may still experience some of the same difficulties they did as children.

In the past, attention deficit disorder was portrayed as a subtype of learning disability. Educators now feel that this is not accurate. Children with attention deficit disorder are often just not *available* for learning. However, many kids who have ADD need academic accommodations for learning disabilities as well.

If not diagnosed and treated, children with ADD may develop significant emotional difficulties, since they are often misunderstood and may feel like failures. The self-esteem of children with ADD is at risk, since many tend to feel criticized and unable to perform well in school.

The causes of attention deficit disorder are still unclear, but most researchers feel that ADD is due to a neurobiological disorder and is not caused by the home or school environments. The *New England Journal of Medicine* published the results of a National Institute of Mental Health study that used advanced brain-imaging techniques (PET scans) to compare the brain metabolism of adults with ADD to those without ADD. It was documented that adults with ADD utilized glucose (the brain's energy source) at a lesser rate than did adults without ADD. The researchers suggested that this reduced brain metabolism rate was greatest in the area of the brain specializing in attention, motor control, and inhibition of responses.

According to the fourth edition of the *Diagnostic and Statistical Man-*

ual of Mental Disorders,* the handbook for diagnosing psychological disorders, attention deficit disorder is divided into three subtypes:

1. Hyperactive-impulsive
2. Inattentive
3. Combined (meeting the criteria for both of the above types)

The criteria for diagnosis of either type are six or more of the symptoms for that type having persisted for at least six months to a degree that is inconsistent with the child's developmental level. And the symptoms must have begun before age seven and occur in two or more settings, such as at school and at home.

Attention Deficit Disorder—Hyperactive-Impulsive Type†

Hyperactivity symptoms:

1. Often fidgets with hands or feet or squirms in seat.
2. Often leaves seat in classroom or in other situations in which remaining seated is expected.
3. Often runs about or climbs excessively in situations in which it is inappropriate (in adolescents or adults, may be limited to subjective feelings of restlessness).
4. Often has difficulty playing or engaging in leisure activities quietly.
5. Is often "on the go" or often acts as if "driven by a motor."
6. Often talks excessively.

Impulsivity symptoms:

7. Often blurts out answers before questions are completed.
8. Often has difficulty awaiting turn.
9. Often interrupts or intrudes on others (for example, butts into conversations or games).

---

*American Psychiatric Association, *Diagnostic and Statistical Manual of Mental Disorders*, 4th ed. (*DSM*-IV) (Washington, D.C.: American Psychiatric Association, 1994), 80.
†American Psychiatric Association, *DSM*-IV, 84.

It is easier to diagnose the youngster with the hyperactive-impulsive type of attention deficit disorder than the inattentive type. Hyperactive kids squirm and fidget, they tend to talk excessively, and move about without apparent forethought. Preschoolers with impulsive hyperactivity intensely display these behaviors, but school-age children seem to tone it down, although it is still difficult for them to remain seated and keep from squirming in their seats. They fidget with almost anything that is in reach of their hands and have a tendency to touch others. The impulsivity is seen as impatience, with the kids interrupting and often blurting out answers before they have been called upon. They tend to have more accidents than other children, such as walking into walls, touching a hot iron, or engaging in potentially dangerous activities without thinking about what could happen.

Jared was brought to my office the first time at age four. His parents, Kevin and Maggie, were distraught because he had been asked to leave his preschool, and it was the second school to do so in a year. Both schools complained that Jared was too aggressive with the other kids, and had difficulty following classroom rules. Naptime was a disaster. He would wiggle and rock his cot so much that he often toppled over onto the floor. Although he loved playing with the other kids, many of them tried to avoid him—where Jared went, so did trouble. His teachers wondered if he was hyperactive and suggested that he be evaluated before being placed in another preschool.

When I met Jared, I was taken by his curiosity and intelligence, as well as his ability to bounce almost nonstop on my couch, at least when we could get him on the couch. The rest of the time he was walking around my office, perusing the various objects, and often interrupting me with a quick "What's that?" or "Who gave you this?" Cute kid, but a real pistol.

After spending a few sessions with Jared, I met with his folks and told them that he was indeed very active and inquisitive, to the point that it distracted him from the task at hand. Whether he was just overactive or truly hyperactive was debatable, though, and I chose to postpone making a diagnosis until he was at least five years old and in kindergarten, as many little kids are impulsive and lacking in self-control during the preschool years, but begin to settle down around the fifth birthday. I suggested placing him in a preschool setting with a very low teacher-to-pupil ratio so that Jared's behavior could be closely monitored.

I helped the teacher at his new school to set up the Smiley Face system (as presented in chapter 6), and Jared's behavior soon became tolerable. On many days, he earned his after-school treat, but several times he brought home sheets with all of the Smileys crossed out. Usually, his misdeeds involved impulsive behaviors—pushing to be first in line, playing too roughly, or engaging in off-task activities (wandering around the room or making noises). Kevin and Maggie felt the behavior management system to be partially successful, but remained concerned about his behavior when he would enter kindergarten in the fall.

The following year turned out to be a repeat performance. His kindergarten teacher found Jared to be more distractible and impulsive than most of her other students and she recommended that he be evaluated for attention deficit disorder.

When I saw Jared this time, he had not learned self-control and his behavior stood out from that of his classmates. I observed him in the classroom, the school library, and the playground, and found that he continued to evidence a significant number of impulsive behaviors in all three settings. His distractibility was interfering with learning and I suggested that the pediatrician be contacted to evaluate the possibility of placing Jared on medication for ADD. This would be in addition to the Smiley Face systems employed both at home and at school.

Jared's pediatrician chose to place him on Ritalin. Although several other medications are commonly used, such as Dexedrine, Cylert, Catapres, and various tricyclic antidepressants, Ritalin tends to have the fewest side effects. Kevin and Maggie started Jared on the medication on a Saturday morning and called me that evening. Even though he was not in school and had few restrictions at home, they saw a significant improvement in his ability to pay attention, comply with requests, and to sit still. One dose of the medication tended to last only three and a half to four hours, but since he was taking it three times a day, his behavior throughout the day had improved significantly. They were excited about the effects this would have when he went to school on Monday.

Like clockwork, I received a telephone call at three-thirty on Monday from Maggie, describing a note written by Jared's teacher. She couldn't believe the change in his ability to sit still and to pay attention. He still tended to be somewhat impulsive and was more fidgety than many of the other kids, but the change was a vast improvement over his prior behavior. I told his family that although this was a good sign, we would have to follow Jared closely and continue using both the medication as well as behavior management. The medication allowed him to stop and think before acting, and the Smiley Face system made it clear which behaviors were appropriate and which weren't, both at school and at home.

I saw Jared and his parents weekly for the next month, and his improvement continued. It was much easier for him to get his homework done because he was completing some of it in school, and he was better able to sit still and finish the rest of it when he returned home. Jared's peer relationships also improved. On the playground, he was not as impulsive, and other kids began to enjoy playing with him. Jared's self-esteem improved as other children initiated activities with him. In one therapy session, he told me that he liked himself better and felt that he was actually smart.

Attention Deficit Disorder—Inattentive Type*

The criteria for diagnosis of ADD-inattentive type are six or more of the following symptoms of inattention having persisted for at least six months to a degree that is inconsistent with the child's developmental level.

1. Often fails to give close attention to details or makes careless mistakes in schoolwork, housework, or other activities.
2. Often has difficulty sustaining attention in tasks or play activities.

---

*American Psychiatric Association, *DSM*-IV, 83.

3. Often does not seem to listen when spoken to directly.
4. Often does not follow through on instructions and fails to finish schoolwork, chores, or duties (not due to oppositional behavior or failure to understand instructions).
5. Often has difficulty organizing tasks and activities.
6. Often avoids, dislikes, or is reluctant to engage in tasks that require sustained mental effort (such as schoolwork or homework).
7. Often loses things necessary for tasks or activities (for example, toys, school assignments, pencils, books, or tools).
8. Is often easily distracted by extraneous stimuli.
9. Is often forgetful in daily activities.

It is difficult to diagnose the child with the inattentive type of attention deficit disorder, especially at a young age. These children do not manifest the impulsivity and misbehavior that kids like Jared (the hyperactive-impulsive type) do. The inattention and distractibility that is characteristic of this type is usually seen only at a later age, in academic situations, for example. These children tend to make careless errors in schoolwork, their work at times is messy, and they have difficulty sustaining attention in both work and play activities. Often they do not appear to have heard what is said, and tasks go uncompleted. It is important, though, to determine whether the child does not complete tasks only because he does not understand the instructions or is willfully noncompliant, or because he truly has ADD. Because school tasks require such sustained mental effort for these kids, many tend to grow to dislike or even avoid academic activities. Pediatricians have found that medication, such as Ritalin, can be very helpful in increasing the ability to focus and the attention span of children with the inattentive type of attention deficit disorder.

Behavioral Techniques for the School Setting

Teachers should work closely with pediatricians, psychologists, and parents of the ADD kid. I believe that a daily reporting system is mandatory in order for the child to realize that his performance and behavior at school are being monitored each day, and that a consequence will follow at home. The teacher can use the Smiley Face system for school (see chapter 6). The child is told that Smileys will be crossed out for inappropriate behaviors such as not completing work, out-of-seat behavior, distracting or touching others, making rude noises, daydreaming excessively, or not completing classwork. If the child does not lose all twelve Smileys (i.e., the last Smiley is not crossed out), she receives a treat each day from her parent. If it is crossed out, no treat is given and a negative consequence, such as going to bed early, occurs that evening. Over the weeks, the number of Smileys on the sheet is lowered, so that the child's behavior must improve in order for her to receive the daily reward.

Many times, I've seen that this system alone works well enough that medication is not necessary, because the child knows that his misbehavior or inattention will be marked and that his parents will find out each day and a consequence given. If his misbehavior or inattention is behavioral in nature (and therefore not true ADD), this should clear it up if the parents are consistent and the consequences are important to the child. Even if the child has ADD, this system will be of help, since it constantly lets the child know what he is doing wrong (e.g., blurting out answers in the classroom or not staying on task) and how close he is coming to either receiving or losing his reward.

Patrick

Our experience began when our son, Patrick, was born. We noticed right from the start that he was different. As an infant, he did not like to be held for long periods of time, he cried quite a bit and was full of energy. As a toddler, his attention span was fairly short. He became frustrated very easily when trying to complete a task and would have tantrums as a result. Soon the whole family began to be affected. It seemed like the whole world revolved around our son. My husband and I began to argue, and my daughter often said she disliked her brother because he was always making trouble. We placed him in preschool, hoping that would help with his behavior. However, this turned into a disaster. The teacher told us that he was being aggressive with other children and not paying attention during class. After four months, we were asked to remove him from the school.

When we first went to see Dr. Peters, my husband and I told her we had no intention of putting Patrick on any kind of medication and hoped that behavior modification and working with the school would correct his problems. We tried putting him on the Smiley Face system, using time-outs and giving rewards, but the situation did not seem to improve. The teacher kept telling us that he was trying so hard but could not seem to help himself. My son would come home from school in tears because he knew that he would be going into "time-out" or losing some more of his toys. Finally, after three months, we discussed the possibility of medication. It was the hardest decision that we ever had to make, but with our son's health and happiness at stake, we decided to give it a try.

WHAT A MIRACLE! We began giving our son Ritalin the week after Thanksgiving. It started working immediately and we saw a total change in his behavior. From day one, he has not been aggressive toward one child, the teacher tells us that he is attentive in class and he raises his hand when he wants to speak. We were concerned that the Ritalin would cause him to act "drugged up," but it didn't. It just helped him to focus and think before reacting. Now when I pick him up from school I no longer have a knot in my stomach waiting for the bad news. Instead, I see a little boy with a big smile telling me what a good day he had.

It should be noted that children with attention deficit disorder do not display all of the symptoms at all times. The behaviors typically worsen when the task requires sustained attention or a great deal of mental effort, or the child is placed in a situation that is not interesting to him, such as listening to lengthy stories or working on repetitive tasks, or in a large group where he may get too wound up. When he is doing something that is fun, involved in a one-on-one situation, or working by himself, the impulsivity, hyperactivity, or inattention may not be seen at all. Working alone, he will be more calm, but in groups, it is more difficult for the impulsive youngster to stay on task because he can get too excited.

What's Ahead for Kids with ADD

Studies have shown that youngsters do not "outgrow" attentional disorders as previously thought. The prognosis will differ depending upon the severity of the attentional problem. Youngsters with mild attentional problems may learn to compensate, and their difficulties may not be evident in their teenage and adult years. However, individuals with severe attentional problems may continue in their teenage and adult years to be much more distractible or inattentive than their peers.

As people with ADD mature, they tend to become less active, impulsive, and distractible, even in severe cases. However, their difficulties may continue to plague them to some degree throughout their lives. Continuation of medication and behavioral management as well as vocational counseling, such as selecting a job with a quiet, calm atmosphere, may be necessary.

The adult may need specific vocational guidelines, if the attentional difficulty is persistent and severe. The distractible individual who chooses a career in law enforcement, for example, may have great difficulty directing traffic at a busy intersection, but may function very well in a less stimulating office situation. Therefore, practical vocational guidance is especially important for teenagers and adults with severe attentional difficulties.

Beyond the elementary and high school levels, many colleges have recently developed programs for individuals with attention deficit disorder. These programs provide a much more structured environment than regular college curricula, and offer tutoring as well.

Several studies have addressed what happens to kids with ADD as they grow to adulthood. In one study, adults who were diagnosed as having ADD as youngsters tended to be more disappointed, pessimistic, and lacking in self-confidence as adults than were those without the disorder (the control group). As a whole, their social skills also tended to be somewhat impaired. However, employers do not seem to be disappointed in adults with ADD, as their high school teachers had been. This may be based in the extreme demands present in the academic situation as compared with the less structured requirements at work.

Gabrielle Weiss and Lily Trokenberg Hechtman's book *Hyperactive Children Grown Up: ADHD in Children, Adolescents, and Adults* notes that in one study, approximately 33 to 50 percent of youngsters with attention deficit disorder continued to have some difficulties in adulthood. These individuals displayed more substance abuse and antisocial behavior than did the control group. In addition, the adults continued to have shorter attention spans, lower impulse control, and more mood swings than did their counterparts. However, Weiss and Hechtman did find that those who were treated with Ritalin as children were less likely to have problems as adults than were those who were not treated with medication as children—perhaps because those who were not treated had poorer self-images and therefore continued to display impulsive or inattentive behaviors throughout childhood.

SINGLE PARENTS AND STEPFAMILIES

As all children tend to profit from structure in the home, so do most parents. In the traditional home (Mom, Dad, and kids), there are two parents making the rules and setting the consequences. But what happens in nontraditional families?

Single parents, either divorced, widowed, or never married, often do not have the support of another adult to discuss things with, nor do they have a shoulder to lean on when they give the child a negative consequence. These single parents face the guilt and their kids' big, sad eyes all on their own. Thus, many single parents cannot stand up to the pressure of giving negative consequences, and so they warn and threaten their kids but rarely move into action with a consequence.

Many divorced singles have told me that it's actually easier to discipline their children now, because the other parent is not there to sabotage their decisions. But others find it's their children having to live under two sets of rules—one at home and one when they visit the ex-spouse—that makes parental consistency difficult. Either way, the kids of single parents need and deserve a behavior management system, perhaps even more so than do kids from two-parent households. Their lives have been disrupted, but new rules may not, as yet, have been developed to replace the old, outdated ones.

Stepparents often find themselves in an even worse situation. Whose rules do we follow? Mine from my last marriage, or yours from your last? Also, stepparenting often involves integrating two sets of kids (originally brought up with two different sets of rules) into one household. Truly a recipe for disaster! Therefore, stepparents need to consider a behavior management system as soon as possible, perhaps even before the nuptials are complete, in order to let each member of the future blended family know what his or her rights and responsibilities are.

This chapter discusses how and why behavior management should be brought into the lives of single parents and stepparents. Taken together, these two types of nontraditional groupings have become even more common in our society than the traditional family, and deserve a discussion of their special needs.

Single Parenting

Most of the more than 2.5 million people who divorce each year are parents, meaning that *millions of kids become children of divorce every year*. Scary thought. Almost 50 percent of kids under the age of eighteen will have lived in a single-parent home sometime during their growing years. Now that's *really* scary!

Studies show that it is how both parents behave during and after the separation and divorce that is the best indicator of their kids' future behavior and mental health. But many parents coming out of a divorce are not emotionally prepared for the changes occurring in their kids. Some folks do a great job, but these are usually parents who had it together before the marital separation. Their kids knew the limits and respected their parents, and the kids felt respected in return. As noted earlier, many intact families never develop that type of healthy respect, and when the family splits, they may have to develop it for the first time. But the single parent faces many other challenges and obstacles to stability—new financial worries, possible depression or guilt feelings, and a sense of loneliness. Many single parents often have so much to worry about personally that it's almost impossible to focus on the kids' needs, at least initially.

Kids may experience many different feelings as their parents are separating and divorcing—denial, anger, embarrassment, shame, guilt, hopelessness, depression, and self-pity. Most children, while they are genuinely concerned about Mom and Dad, are worried primarily about what is going to happen to them. "Will I be able to fall asleep at Dad's house?" or "Will I still get birthday presents now that Mom and Dad don't live together?" And let's not forget that many little kids continue to harbor hope that their folks will get back together again in the future. I've seen several children in my practice who insist that their parents will work it out, even after both have remarried and have children in their new relationships!

However, once the dust settles and a semblance of emotional stability returns to the family, what can a single parent do to keep kids on track? How about becoming the benevolent dictator I discussed in chapter 5? Single parents need to be fair, yet in control. These folks usually do not have the support of another committed adult to back them up, to take over when they feel like strangling a child, or to listen to their problems and to suggest alternatives. Grandparents are generally quite helpful, but many single parents do not live near their folks, or Grandma and Grandpa are just not available to help out.

Janice and Rory are typical clients. They had recently separated and were having difficulty controlling their five- and six-year-old daughters, Allyn and Jordan. Janice believed in setting up and following rules for the kids, but Rory was reluctant to do so. He told me at a session that he felt guilty disciplining the girls during a visit since he saw them only twice a week now.

I tried to impress upon both parents that setting up a behavior management system would be in everyone's best interest, and that the temporary guilt feelings that go hand in hand with giving negative consequences were a normal part of the process. Janice was able to comply with the program, but Rory remained inconsistent, and the girls played him like a fiddle.

Janice was concerned that this would confuse the kids or allow them to be manipulative ("Dad doesn't make us clean our rooms— he's nicer than you!"), but I assured her that this would not occur and not to worry about Rory's handling of the kids. Kids are smart, and once they realize what the rules and consequences are, they usually comply. How Rory wanted his relationship with his kids to be was his concern, not hers. She was responsible only for the way she expected them to behave when they were with her.

A trap that many residential or custodial parents often fall into is taking psychological responsibility for their ex-spouse's relationship with the kids. Not only may your ex not want your help, but he may actually view it as interference. If your ex was uninvolved with the kids while you were married, most likely this lack of involvement will continue in the future, especially if it's now inconvenient to see the children. And if your ex was not good at disciplining the children before the divorce, the same attitude will most likely prevail in the new living situation.

If you set up a Smiley Face system in your home, it will work even though your ex may be a "Disney World parent," with weekend visits becoming a behavioral free-for-all with few expectations of the kids. The children will respect you and your rules, and whether they respond to your ex is *not your responsibility,* nor your problem. You may need to post this statement on your bathroom mirror to remind yourself if guilt feelings begin to creep up on you!

Another problem unique to single-parent households is that the ex-spouse rarely becomes an ex-parent. To many single parents, it feels like a life sentence having to deal with someone who makes you so uncomfortable that you couldn't live together any longer, but you still have to work together regarding the children. On the other hand, some single parents enjoy having the ex-spouse available for the kids, because it gives both parent and child a needed break.

Realistically, though, most divorced folks I know continue their bitterness way beyond the final court hearing, and the animosity may continue to color their lives forever. Many nonresidential or noncustodial parents become inconsistent in seeing their kids, which is painful for the children, disruptive to the residential parent, and tends to lead to poor kid self-esteem and much bitterness on the part of the residential parent.

Children living with single parents quickly learn how to take advantage of the situation. Most of these kids soon pick up on the guilt that you feel for the disruption of their original home. Their kid radar also catches your depression, moods, and anger. And what would any normal kid who has his parent in this position do? Well, let's see:

* Play the poor divorced kid role: "Don't expect much from me, I've been hurt, you know."
* Catch you when you are confused or overloaded and ask for a privilege you normally wouldn't allow. You may give in because it's too tough to deal with him at that moment, and you can't send him to the next room to ask his father for a decision.
* Go in for the kill: "If you don't buy me a new toy, I'm going to live with Mom!"

Smart kid, dumb parent, if you go along with this stuff. Never, never underestimate how perceptive children can be. Often they know what you're feeling even before you've figured it out! Remember, our kids have more energy than we do and maybe even more smarts (although less experience), and they just never seem to give up on what they want.

So is the benevolent dictatorship starting to sound a little bit better to you? I hope so, because it will save your sanity and that of your children. The best way to start a benevolent dictatorship is to begin a behavior management plan immediately. Single parents need their homes to work like clockwork, because there's only one of you to help organize and make sure that everyone is fed, bathed, and makes it to bed on time. Kids who dawdle, have their own agenda, or outright disobey their parents throw a wrench into the system. Everything stops as you cajole, nag, and demand that something get done, and if that child is just poky or directly ornery, the whole family pays.

To stop this, use the Smiley Face system. It may be difficult to stick to because there's only one parent, but, on the other hand, there's no other adult there to sabotage your plan. If Grandma or another adult is frequently involved, try to convince her to use the program also so that the kids learn to show respect in different situations.

Unfair as it may seem, I'm asking you, as a single parent, to start a behavior management system that is harder to do because you're alone. But if you don't set up fair rules and have consequences tied to your children's behavior, your house may truly become chaotic. If it is already, let's stop the cycle and get back to the control you deserve as a parent.

Quiz Time

Okay, it's time for a soul-searching checkup! You know that you should make some changes in your personal life and family dynamics if you agree with many of these statements:

1. You feel that your kids are running the show and that they cooperate only when they want something from you.
2. You see two-parent families and are envious of the support they appear to give to each other. You feel alone and over-whelmed by all the responsibility you've taken on.
3. You feel guilty for the divorce because of the changes your kids have had to endure. To assuage your guilt, you give in to their demands.
4. You wake up many weekend mornings feeling as if it's just not worth it, stay in your pajamas all day, and let the kids fend for themselves.
5. You need help. There's only one of you and three kids to raise. You're afraid to ask your ex to take the kids more often in order to give you a break. You feel that you should be able to handle it all yourself.
6. You bad-mouth your ex-spouse whenever you see an opening to do so.
7. You find yourself buying in to your daughter's victim mentality and excuse her from responsibilities because she now comes from a broken home.
8. You work full-time at a job all day and keep house full-time all evening, while your kids do very little to help out. You don't push it because you know they'll hassle you, and you're just not up for it right now.
9. You walk on eggshells around your kids and ex-spouse.
10. You've had it. You realize that you deserve a life!

Now—how about some suggestions for keeping your kids mentally healthy through this change in their lives?

1. Don't bad-mouth the other parent in your kid's presence, and also watch it when you're talking on the telephone. Kids hear that kind of stuff but become selectively deaf when you ask for help with the groceries.

2. When your kid speaks angrily about the other parent, just listen. You can try making suggestions to help, but don't add anything to your child's list of crimes committed by the other parent.

3. Keep your kids out of the middle. If you need information (dates, times, medical data), go directly to the other parent.

4. Do not grill your kid for information about the other parent—it will only lead to frustration and aggravation. An exception is information that may affect your child's safety while at the other home.

5. Encourage your child to cooperate on visits with the nonresidential or noncustodial parent. It may be boring over there, and he may not feel close to his mom or dad, but barring neglect or abuse, the child should honor the visitation.

6. *Move on—get a life.* If you find yourself still obsessing about your "ex" son-of-a-gun, realize that he is still controlling your life. Now how does *that* make you feel?

Stepparenting

The number of stepfamilies in America has blossomed since the 1970s. The Stepfamily Foundation quotes the following statistics:

* Approximately 35 percent of American children currently live in a step relationship (child and parent with a partner who is not the child's biological parent).

* It is predicted that 60 percent of children born today will spend part of their life in a single-family household and in one or more step relationships.

* More than 70 million Americans are currently involved in step relationships.

* It is predicted that 75 percent of all step relationships will break up. The major cause of these breakups are child- and step-related issues.

Your kid's personality does not change magically when you walk down the aisle for that second or even third time. A reasonable child stays reasonable, and a manipulator continues to play chess (but with people as pawns). So what's different? Why do the majority of remarriages with kids involved end in divorce within five years after the remarriage?

I believe it is due mainly to both spouses' naïve expectations of what the new family should be like. My practice is heavily weighted with stepfamilies, and I've found that both spouses hope that the stepfamily will follow the rules of each one's original home, somehow magically blending both sets of rules together. It astonishes me when both parents bring kids into the situation and expect them to deal smoothly not only with a new stepparent, but also with stepsiblings who either visit or live with them. These expectations are not only naïve, but they are generally wrong, and therefore put undue pressure on all family members to behave in ways that they are not ready for.

Over the years, I've pondered the question of how such intelligent people can have such naïve ideas about stepparenting. I've concluded that most rely on their experiences with the kids while they were dating. Often children are more accepting of Dad's girlfriend than they are when she becomes his new wife for two main reasons: she hasn't taken their mother's place yet, and most likely as a girlfriend she was not trying to discipline them. However, once there is a wedding, kids' perceptions of the new stepparent often change drastically. Many children have described to me how much fun the wedding was and how nice they felt their stepparent was before living together, but now think quite differently since Dad's handed her some control of the family.

If you are in a stepfamily, there are many issues to be dealt with.
* Some previously childless spouses have never had to deal with the idiosyncrasies of kids before.

* Stepkids often reject *any* disciplinary attempts by a new step-parent, no matter how kind the stepparent is.
* Deciding who disciplines whose children is often chaotic. Rules tend to change depending upon the parent's mood or whose kid did the crime.
* Your child now has to share you with someone other than her natural parent, and even if she does like him, she may feel disloyal to her natural father by admitting that Stepdad's not so bad after all.

Although there are no easy answers to these dilemmas, there are some starting points. First, try to understand where your kid is coming from. A child in a stepfamily has to learn the ropes of at least three different households—the original nuclear family, the single-parent home, and now sharing her parent with a person whom she might not even like.

The only way to begin to make sense of this is to keep the lines of communication open. At least if your daughter can feel safe letting you know how she feels about Stepdad and his visiting or live-in kids, she'll realize that you do care. You may not be able to change many things, but kids need to know that you're trying. The tough part is getting her to understand your position—how being in the middle sometimes makes you feel like baloney in a sandwich, about to be eaten alive by both sides.

The next step is to set up a new structure for the family, and this is where the key word for stepfamilies comes in: *compromise*. For instance, if Stepdad handled discipline in his original family and you left most of it to your ex-spouse, it's only natural for the two of you to try the same routine with your new family. Sounds reasonable, doesn't it? But it's not—your children may have accepted discipline from their natural father, but they're probably not going to listen to this man, whom you picked out, who takes away your time from them, and who has basically upset the balance of power in the family. If your child was a bit tyrannical before, you can be sure that he won't appreciate one inch of his turf disturbed!

Most stepfamilies profit from a behavioral system because it establishes *one set* of rules for the household and is usually less confusing than the parents' previous attempts to blend two sets of rules into one. I'm not saying that your kid will like the idea of going on the Smiley Face system and receiving consequences for her behavior—in fact, she'll probably balk at it. But you really have little choice. I can practically guarantee that if your new family does not sit down together and compromise on chores, which behaviors are acceptable and which are not, and what rewards and punishments all of the kids will receive, then your home will most likely be chaotic, and your children will perceive it as an unfair situation.

Putting all of the kids (yours, mine, and ours) on such a program is the only way to keep the rules clear and fair. Sure, the kids will gripe, "We didn't have to do this before you married Chad, so why do we have to do it now?" The only respectable answer is something like "Because I am married to Chad, he is your stepfather, and we are going to follow the house rules. They're not just for you, but for your stepbrothers and your half sister also. It's as fair as I can make it, and that's that!"

Sound a bit harsh? Perhaps so. But it's a lot better than the chaos that will occur if you don't agree on family rules and stick to the consequences. Remember, a majority of stepfamilies divorce, mainly because of disagreements over kid issues.

It's important that Stepdad follow the rules, too, crossing out Smiley Faces for rude behavior and also giving out the treats that were earned. Sure, you'll hear, "He's not my father. He can't cross out a Smiley Face." The solution is to have Stepdad use the chart even more. You'll probably get lots of "I'm going to live with Dad. He doesn't have a chart and I won't have to put up with Stepdad!" Try not to get suckered into that one. Most likely your child is angry at the moment, and it will pass. If you're foolish enough to bite, well, you'll be blackmailed for a long time as your kid asserts his control over your new family.

Most important, don't allow the kids to engage in "splitting" behavior—if Stepdad says no, get Mom to say yes, possibly by omitting some important information. Then get out the Legos and watch the folks go at it. The couple's relationship should remain a priority, and splitting will demoralize you and cause you to question why you complicated your life with a new spouse. You probably remarried for many good reasons—love, security, and a better situation for your kids. Too bad that engagement rings don't come with a crystal ball so that you can weigh the new comforts against the inevitable conflicts.

Some realistic rules for stepparents that I've developed over the years are:

1. Try not to be defensive and judgmental. It doesn't work and saps your emotional energy.
2. To be respected by your stepkids, you need to learn to respect them.
3. Understand that while you are responsible for providing a safe, wholesome environment for your stepchild, the ultimate responsibility for developing her moral character lies with her natural parent.
4. Encourage your stepkid's relationship with the natural parent. Do not say negative things about him or her.
5. Watch that you show no favoritism toward your own kids (your stepchild has a built-in "sonar frequency band" to pick up on this and won't miss a thing).
6. Don't expect your stepkids to love you, even if you love them. True love takes lots of time to develop. Settle for respectful behavior right now, and perhaps love will come later.
7. Encourage your new spouse to spend time with his or her kids alone. They may have had their parent all to themselves, and now they have to share with you.
8. Stepparents who try to be both parent and friend can be successful. There's nothing wrong with the kids calling you by your first name, but you are a parent first and a friend second.

Quiz Time

You know you're in trouble as a parent in a stepfamily if you answer yes to many of these items:

1. You're realizing that the kids who were friendly to you when you were dating their parent have become resentful when you now try to discipline them.
2. You assumed that this new family would immediately and automatically function smoothly since things went so well before you married and began living together.
3. You believe that everyone will grow to love one another (and quickly, too).
4. You feel that what you experienced in your first family is irrelevant now. The old customs will be erased, and you will start all new family traditions immediately.
5. You think that discipline will be a cinch—"I've never been good at it, so I'll let my new wife discipline all of the kids. She seems to do a better job of raising the children, although she's been losing her cool lately, but let's just give it some time. I'm too busy working to discipline anyhow!"
6. You wonder if you've made the wrong decision about remarriage. It seems like the kids (and maybe you) were happier and lived a simpler life before getting rehitched.
7. You resent your new spouse's uninvolvement with your kids. It seemed different when you were dating, but after the dust settled, it's as if you have two relationships: one with your spouse and one with your children.
8. It seems as if there's rarely any time for just the two of you. Somehow keeping a date together always seems to get sabotaged.
9. You're sick and tired of being in the middle of arguments between your spouse and your kids. You're considering locking all of them in a padded room and letting them "duke it out" together.
10. Your ex is beginning to look better and better to you as time goes by.

If yes was your response to many of these questions, please don't throw in the towel. Stepparenting can be the most challenging of all family setups, and it takes a special kind of patience, persistence, love, and a lot of maturity to survive.

What to do? Convene a family meeting in order to set up the Smiley Face system. The kids' behavior and attitudes will improve. After ten days, decide what still needs to be changed—and continue to use communication and family meetings to try to tackle new problems as they come up. Remember, though, nothing will help if you allow the kids to "split" you and your spouse. They need to see that you are committed to the marital relationship and are going to work together as a united team, not against the kids but with them. Back each other up, while still listening to the children and trying to be as fair as possible.

THE EFFECTIVE PARENT

O ver the years, I've come to realize that it helps to look at parenting from the big-picture perspective. The day-to-day annoyances, disciplinary actions, and furious looks from your child are expected, although unpleasant, parts of the child-raising process. This stuff comes and goes, but what really counts is how your kids turn out as teenagers and as young adults. Do they take responsibility for their actions? Can they accept constructive criticism and make the necessary changes? Do they respect you and are they respected by others in return?

The best guarantee that your little one will grow to learn responsibility and self-control is to provide him with clear guidelines to live by. *And it's never too soon to begin the process!* The key points to remember are:

1. *Be consistent.* If you set up a rule, follow it.
2. *Quit threatening—use action.* A twenty-minute time-out for a five-year-old often gets the kid's attention and promotes correct decision making the next time around.
3. *Put some teeth in the consequences.* If it really doesn't bother your child, the consequence is probably not going to work. Ten minutes of bedroom time-out pales in comparison with thirty minutes of bathroom time-out.
4. *Make the rule–consequence connection very clear and comprehensive.*

Remember, gray areas and ambiguity allow kids to argue that they really didn't understand the rule to begin with.

5. *Don't expect your child to be reasonable.* If he or she is, great, take it. But most kids have a hard time seeing things your way. Just because they don't feel that a rule is fair doesn't mean that you can't insist upon it. If it's important to you, then it's important to the family.

6. *Avoid winning the battle and losing the war.* You may need to let some of the small stuff go (wanting to wear the same shirt two days in a row) and focus upon issues that will mold your child's life (school grades, politeness, values and morals).

7. *Don't expect yourself to be reasonable all the time.* No matter how much you try, there will be days when you are unfair to the kids. Try to ascertain why you are in a bad mood and do something to stop it. If nothing works, explain to your kids what's going on and let them know that you are trying to get back on an even keel.

8. *Have a game plan for times when you can't use the typical consequence for your child's inappropriate behavior.* Be prepared to leave the mall early, turn the car around if the kids won't stop fighting, or use outside help such as a chat with the school principal if the usual consequences don't seem to be working.

9. *Be prepared to use nontraditional consequences if your regular ones seem to be losing their effectiveness.* Giving away a possession usually gets your child's attention—and changes his behavior. Be creative. If one tactic doesn't work, try a new one. Remember, you are the parent and really do have more power and control over the home situation than your kids do. It may not seem so at times, but that's because they are challenging you to see if you'll dig in your heels and stand firm or if you'll cave in.

10. *Think of your child's happiness and fulfillment as a long-term goal, not a short-term fix.* A child who grows up understanding his place in the grand scheme of this world will naturally know how to fit in and to successfully deal with his employer, spouse, coworkers, and, yes, even his own kids. Most likely, he will be

content and happy. A child who is not given the gift of self-discipline will have to learn limit setting the hard way—perhaps through the judicial system.

If you not only follow these key points, but also inculcate them into the very being of your parenting persona, most likely your kids will turn out to be just fine. The tyranny of the terrible twos will gradually melt into a more reasonable stance if your children believe that you love them more than anything else in the world, but that you will not tolerate selfishness or disrespect. If you are consistent, they'll get the message. Some ornery critters may take longer than others to get the drift, but over time your message will sink in! It's definitely worth the effort and patience needed. After all, there's nothing more thrilling than the realization that your once difficult, egocentric three-year-old has now blossomed into a sensitive, responsible, caring young lady who's not only the apple of your eye, but confident and proud of herself. That makes all of the time, involvement, and, yes, the work of parenting, well worth it!

Parenting Resources

Ch.A.D.D. (Children and Adults with Attention Deficit
   Disorder)
499 Northwest 70th Avenue
Suite 101
Plantation, FL 33717
954-587-3700

PURPOSE: Provides resources for parents of children with attention
deficit disorder. Offers support groups as well as many educational
and counseling publications.

Community Mental Health Centers
(Check your local listing)

PURPOSE: Offers counseling, testing, and family therapy.

Joy Schools (Richard and Linda Eyre)
1516 Foothill Dr.
Salt Lake City, UT 84108
801-581-0112

PURPOSE: Provides parents with a curriculum for teaching social and
emotional skills to preschoolers.

Parents Without Partners
401 North Michigan Avenue
Chicago, IL 60611-4267
800-637-7974

PURPOSE: To promote the study of and to alleviate the problems of single parents in relation to the welfare and upbringing of their children and the acceptance into the general social order of single parents and their children.

Single Mothers by Choice
P.O. Box 1642
Gracie Square Station
New York, NY 10028
212-988-0993

PURPOSE: Provides support for single mothers (does not include mothers who are widowed or divorced), disseminates information to women who choose to be single parents.

Stepfamily Foundation
333 West End Avenue
New York, NY 10023
212-877-3244

PURPOSE: To counsel and inform stepfamilies throughout the world and to train professionals. Information available twenty-four hours (212-799-STEP) as well as twenty-four-hour hot line (212-744-6924).

Listed below are free brochures available from the American Academy of Pediatrics:

Allergies in Children: Plain Talk for Parents
Bed-wetting
Child Care: What's Best for Your Family

Child Sexual Abuse: What It Is and How to Prevent It
Divorce and Children
Growing Up Healthy: Fat, Cholesterol, and More
Healthy Communication with Your Child
Healthy Start: Feeding Kids Right Isn't Always Easy
Healthy Start: Tips for Preventing Food Hassles
A Parent's Guide to Water Safety
Playground Safety
Prevent Shaken Baby Syndrome fact sheet
Raising Children to Resist Violence
Right from the Start: ABC's of Good Nutrition
Single Parenting
Sleep Problems in Children
Sports and Your Child
Starting Solid Foods
Television and the Family
Temper Tantrums
Thumbs, Fingers, and Pacifiers
Toilet Training
Toy Safety
Understanding the ADHD Child: Information for Parents about Attention-Deficit/Hyperactivity Disorder
What's to Eat?: Healthy Foods for Hungry Children
Your Child and the Environment
Your Child's Growth: Developmental Milestones

When ordering these free brochures, please send a self-addressed, stamped business-size envelope to:

> Name of brochure requested
> Dept. C
> P.O. Box 927
> Elk Grove Village, IL 60009-0927

References and Suggested Reading

Adler, Allan J., and Christine Archambault. *Divorce Recovery: Healing the Hurt Through Self-Help and Professional Support.* Washington, D.C.: PIA Press, 1991.

Albert, Linda. *Coping with Kids.* New York: Ballantine Books, 1984.

Albert, Linda, and Michael Popkin. *Quality Parenting: How to Transform the Everyday Moments We Spend with Our Children into Special, Meaningful Time.* New York: Random House, 1987.

American Psychiatric Association. *Diagnostic and Statistical Manual of Mental Disorders.* 4th ed. Washington, D.C.: American Psychiatric Association, 1994.

Ames, Louise Bates, and Frances L. Ilg. *Your Six-Year-Old: Loving and Defiant.* New York: Dell, 1981.

————. *Your Four-Year-Old: Wild and Wonderful.* New York: DTP, 1989.

————. *Your Three-Year-Old: Friend or Enemy.* New York: Delacorte, 1993.

————. *Your Two-Year-Old: Terrible or Tender.* New York: Delacorte, 1993.

————. *Your Five-Year-Old: Sunny and Serene.* New York: Delacorte, 1995.

————. *Your One-Year-Old: The Fun-Loving, Fussy 12- to 24-Month-Old.* New York: Doubleday, 1995.

Barkley, Russell A. *Hyperactive Children: A Handbook for Diagnosis and Treatment.* New York: Guilford Press, 1981.

————. *Attention-Deficit Hyperactivity Disorder: A Handbook for Diagnosis and Treatment.* New York: Guilford Press, 1990.

Belli, Melvin M., and Mel Krantzler. *Divorcing.* New York: St. Martin's Press, 1990.

Bernstein, Anne C. *Yours, Mine, and Ours: How Families Change When Remarried Parents Have a Child Together.* New York: W. W. Norton & Company, 1990.

Bodenhamer, Gregory. *Back in Control: How to Get Your Children to Behave.* Englewood Cliffs, NJ: Prentice Hall, 1983.

Brazelton, T. Berry. *Touchpoints: Your Child's Emotional and Behavioral Development.* Reading, MA: Addison-Wesley, 1994.

Ch.A.D.D. Education Committee. *Attention Deficit Disorders: A Guide for Teachers.* Plantation, FL: Ch.A.D.D., 1988.

Clark, Lynn. *The Time-Out Solution: A Parent's Guide for Handling Everyday Behavioral Problems.* Chicago: NTC/Contemporary Books, 1989.

Conners, C. Keith. *Hyperkinetic Children: A Neuropsychosocial Approach.* Beverly Hills: Sage Publications, 1986.

Davis, Julie. "Reconcilable Differences." *Child* (October 1990): 59–73.

Dobson, James. *Dare to Discipline.* New York: Bantam Books, 1982.

————. *The New Dare to Discipline.* Wheaton, IL: Tyndale House Publishers, 1996.

Dodson, Fitzhugh. *How to Discipline with Love: From Crib to College.* New York: New American Library, 1978.

Elkind, David. *The Hurried Child: Growing Up Too Fast Too Soon.* Reading, MA: Addison-Wesley, 1989.

————. *Ties That Stress: The New Family Imbalance.* Cambridge, MA: Harvard University Press, 1995.

Faber, Adele, and Elaine Mazlish. *How to Talk So Kids Will Listen and Listen So Kids Will Talk.* New York: Avon Books, 1991.

————. *Siblings Without Rivalry: How to Help Your Children Live Together So You Can Live Too.* New York: Avon Books, 1998.

Friedman, Ronald J., and Guy T. Doyal. *Attention Deficit Disorder and Hyperactivity.* 2nd ed. Danville, Illinois: The Interstate Publishing, 1987.

Goleman, Daniel. *Emotional Intelligence.* New York: Bantam Books, 1997.

Harper, Timothy. "Labeled—but Disabled?" *Sky* magazine (September 1996): 87–93.

Ingersoll, Barbara. *Your Hyperactive Child: A Parent's Guide to Coping with Attention Deficit Disorder.* New York: Main Street Books, 1988.

Kagan, Jerome. *Nature of the Child.* New York: Basic Books, 1994.

Lavin, Paul. *Parenting the Overactive Child: Alternatives to Drug Therapy.* New York: Madison Books, 1990.

Lofas, Jeannette, and Dawn Sova. *Stepparenting: Everything You Need to Know to Make It Work.* New York: Kensington Publishing, 1995.

Magid, Ken, and Carole A. McKelvey. *High-Risk: Children Without a Conscience.* New York: Bantam Books, 1990.

Neifert, Marianne. "It's Potty Time!" *Parenting* (August 1996): 66–72.

Peck, M. Scott. *The Road Less Traveled: A New Psychology of Love, Traditional Values and Spiritual Growth.* New York: Touchstone, 1988.

Pipher, Mary. *Reviving Ophelia: Saving the Selves of Adolescent Girls.* New York: Ballantine Books, 1995.

Ricci, Isolina. *Mom's House, Dad's House: A Complete Guide for Parents Who Are Separated, Divorced, or Remarried.* New York: Fireside, 1997.

Rimm, Sylvia. *Dr. Sylvia Rimm's Smart Parenting: How to Parent So Children Will Learn.* New York: Crown Publishing Group, 1997.

Rosemond, John. *Parent Power! A Common-Sense Approach to Parenting in the '90s and Beyond.* Kansas City: Andrews and McMeel, 1991.

Rubenstein, Mark. "What Children Fear the Most." *Child* (July/August 1989): 42.

Sammons, William. "Baby, Don't Cry!" *Child* (September/October 1989): 102–10.

Savage, Karen, and Patricia Adams. *The Good Stepmother: A Survival Guide.* New York: Avon Books, 1989.

Silverman, Marvin, and David Lustig. *Parent Survival Training.* North Hollywood: Wilshire Book Company, 1987.

Thomas, Alexander, and Stella Chess. "What Is Temperament?" *Child Development* 58 (1987): 505–29.

Weiss, Gabrielle, and Lily Trokenberg Hechtman. *Hyperactive Children Grown Up: ADHD in Children, Adolescents, and Adults.* New York: Guilford Press, 1993.

Wender, Paul H. *The Hyperactive Child, Adolescent, and Adult: Attention Deficit Disorder Through the Lifespan.* New York: Oxford University Press, 1987.

Zametkin, A. J., et al. "Cerebral Glucose Metabolism in Adults with Hyperactivity of Childhood Onset." *New England Journal of Medicine* 323(20) (November 15, 1990): 1361–66.

Ziglar, Zig. *Raising Positive Kids in a Negative World.* New York: Ballantine Books, 1996.

Acknowledgments

With sincere appreciation to the families who have placed their children in my hands as we worked toward resolving the day-to-day problems and the major traumas. Together we grew and learned, and this book is based on the insights gained.

Thanks to the special crew at Golden Books: Laura Yorke, Cassie Jones, Bob Asahina, Meredith Greene, and all the folks that made it happen. Appreciation to Jan Miller, who brought me to Golden, and Jean Loveland, who put the finishing touches on the manuscript.

And another round of hugs and kisses to Tim and the kids . . . forever.

INDEX

About the Author

Dr. Ruth Peters is a clinical psychologist who specializes in treating children and adolescents in her private practice in Clearwater, Florida. She teaches parents how to regain control of their difficult children and how to motivate kids to reach their academic potential. She is a consultant to Sylvan Learning Centers and a parenting contributor to *Good Morning America* and has been featured frequently on *Oprah, Good Morning America, CBS This Morning, Today,* and numerous other talk shows. She has been a contributing editor to *Child* magazine and currently writes a column for the *St. Petersburg Times* called "Middle Ground" that focuses on the problems of parenting adolescents. She is the author of *Don't Be Afraid to Discipline* and an audiotape parenting program, "The Successful Child." Dr. Peters lives in Clearwater, Florida, with her husband and two children.